The Ultimate Dandelion Cookbook

148 Recipes for
Dandelion Leaves, Flowers, Buds, Stems, & Roots

by
Kristina Seleshanko

D1694225

Table of Contents

Why Dandelions?

What would you think if someone told you one of the world's most nutritious foods was also tasty, could be cooked many different ways, was easy to find, and was totally free? I know what I'd do: I'd run out and grab some! Well, the good news is, there *is* such a food: Dandelions.

Right now, some of you are crinkling your noses and saying, "Ick!" Others probably think I've gone crazy. But it's true. Dandelions, those pesky weeds with bright yellow flowers that you've grown up thinking are the enemy of perfect lawns, tidy sidewalks, and weed-free flower beds? They are actually food.

Dandelions aren't native to North America. They were actually *brought* here – on purpose – by immigrants who knew what valuable food they are. In fact, dandelions have an important place in American culinary history. They helped keep the early settlers alive; they made the pioneers more healthy; they even helped make family food budgets stretch further during The Great Depression and World War II.

But somehow, after the war, the role of dandelions in the North American diet declined. As super-grocery stores packed with a wide variety of foods became the norm, more people put off dandelions for more "modern" fare like soup in a red and white can and macaroni and cheese in a blue box.

Happily, today wholesome food is making a come back. Gourmet restaurants serve up dandelion greens (but rarely other parts of the plant), charging hefty sums. Health food stores carry dandelion leaves throughout most of the year. High end grocers do, too. You can even buy dandelion seeds from some of the nation's best home gardening seed suppliers. But you don't have to spend lots of cash to enjoy the nutritious goodness of dandelion leaves, flowers, buds, stems, and roots. You can take advantage of this super food for the mere cost of taking a few minutes to pick and wash it.

I think you'll be pleasantly surprised by all you can do in the kitchen with dandelions. Whether you want to make salads, soups, quiche, noodles, enchiladas, pickles, ice cream, or cookies…You can use dandelions.

Bon appetite!

Kristina

P.S. Do you love the idea of getting healthy, wild, free food? Check out the "Foraging" section on my blog for articles about other types of wild plants that make good food:
http://www.proverbsthirtyonewoman.blogspot.com/search/label/Foraging

Tips for Cooking with Dandelions

Buying Dandelions

Dandelions grow almost everywhere, but if you're having trouble finding them growing wild (which can happen if the soil is *really* poor), take heart! Dandelions – mostly leaves – are available at many health food stores, gourmet markets, farmer's markets, and upscale grocery stores. You can also find dehydrated or freeze dried dandelion leaves online, as well as dehydrated dandelion roots. And, although I laugh every time I see them, you can buy dandelion seeds from many seed catalogs, including one of my favorites, Territorial Seed.

Picking Free Dandelions

Part of the joy of dandelions is how plentiful they are - and how easy they are to identify. That said, there are two rules everyone should follow when foraging for dandelions:

1. Never harvest dandelions near roadways, where the plants soak up chemical fumes, or from any location where chemical sprays (such as weed killers) may be used.

2. Always positively identify any wild plant before eating it.

Happily, none of the dandelion's look-alikes are dangerous to eat. When you think you've found a dandelion plant, look for these key features:

1. Tooth-shaped, hairless leaves.

2. Leaves and stems growing directly from the rootstalk in the soil.

3. One flower per stem.

4. Stems without branches on them.

5. A milky white sap when a stem is broken.

6. A thick root, looking rather like a small parsnip. Growing off this main root may be smaller, hair-like roots.

Quick Notes on the Recipes

Serving Size & Yields: All yields and serving sizes are approximate. Variations depend upon whether the dish is used as a side or main dish, the appetite of the eaters, and – sometimes – the quantity of dandelion or other ingredients used.

Cooked vs. Raw: When reading the recipes, it's important to understand that if a recipe reads

½ cup dandelion leaves, cooked

the leaves should be measured raw, then cooked (not cooked and then measured).

Dandelion leaves vs. Dandelion greens: Most commonly, you'll hear dandelion leaves called "dandelion greens" in restaurants, grocery stores, and cookbooks. However, in this cookbook I divided the recipes according to what part of the dandelion they use; therefore, I chose to use the term "dandelion leaves" throughout.

Dandelion Leaves: A Super Food

When we think of dark, leafy greens that are good for us, most people think of spinach, kale, or maybe collards. But dandelion leaves compete with these more popular greens – sometimes even coming out ahead of them. For example, they beat out spinach in terms of protein, vitamins A, C, K, Omega 6, iron, phosphorus, potassium, and calcium.

Per Serving, Raw

	Dandelion leaves	Spinach	Kale	Collards
Calories	25	7	33	11
Carbohydrate	5 g	1 g	7 g	2 g
Protein	1.5 g	1 g	2 g	1 g
Vitamin A	5588 IU	2813 IU	10302 IU	2400 IU
Vitamin C	19.3 mg	8.4 mg	80.4 mg	12.7 mg
Vitamin K	428 mcg	145 mcg	547 mcg	184 mcg
Folate	14.9 mcg	58.2 mcg	19.4 mcg	59.8 mcg
Omega 3	24.2 mg	41.4 mg	121 mg	38.9 mg
Omega 6	144 mg	7.8 mg	92.4 mg	29.5 mg
Calcium	103 mg	29.7 mg	90.5 mg	52.2 mg
Iron	1.7 mg	.8 mg	1.1 mg	.1 mg
Magnesium	19.8 mg	23.7 mg	22.8 mg	3.2 mg
Phosphorus	36.3 mg	14.7 mg	37.5 mg	3.6 mg
Potassium	218 mg	167 mg	299 mg	60.8 mg

Flavor

Dandelion leaves taste a lot like other leafy greens, especially collards, but have a slightly more bitter flavor. However, if the leaves are harvested early in the spring, before buds appear on the plant, th*ey aren't as bitter as many popular salad greens*. Cooking the leaves also reduces or completely takes away the bitterness.

When to Harvest Dandelion Leaves

The window in which dandelion leaves are naturally tasty and not too bitter is short. You must catch the plant *before* it sends out buds. If you live where snow is the winter norm, start looking for dandelion leaves as soon as the snow melts. In warmer regions, begin looking around November or December. Take advantage of the dandelion's short season by harvesting as many leaves as you can, preserving them for future use. (Keep reading for specific information on how to do this.)

If you miss the natural time frame for harvesting dandelion leaves, all is not lost. You may:

1. Pick the dandelion leaves anyway, then bring a pot of water to a boil. Add the leaves and simmer for 3 minutes or until tender. Taste. If the leaves still seem bitter, repeat with fresh water. This removes much of the bitterness, but also some of the dandelion's nutrients.

2. Cut off all the dandelion leaves, stems, buds, and flowers at the soil level and allow the plant to re-grow. Some people also cover the plant with a box, bowl, or other object that completely blocks out the sun. The new leaves will be almost as good as early spring leaves - but if the plant is covered, the nutritional content will be slightly reduced.

3. If the leaves are still youngish, but the plant has sent up stems and buds, try soaking the leaves in salt water, as the French do. Or, use apple cider vinegar or lemon juice.

4. Wait until fall. After a couple of hard frosts, most of the bitterness will disappear from the leaves.

5. Pull up one or more plants by the roots. (For tips on doing this, see the chapter on dandelion roots.) Pot the plants. Cut back all the leaves, stems, and flowers. Bring the pot indoors before the first hard frost and place near a sunny window. When new leaves emerge, harvest them right away. Keep doing this, and you'll have a continual supply of good dandelion leaves.

Buying Dandelion Leaves

Some health food stores, farmer's markets, and upscale grocery stores carry dandelion leaves nearly year round. These dandelions are primarily grown in green houses, and new crops are sowed throughout the year so the leaves never become too bitter. Look for dandelion leaves that are a dark green, without blemish, not wilted, and not enormous in size.

Preserving Dandelion Leaves

Dandelion leaves may be preserved through freezing, dehydrating, or canning.

Freezing: Fill a clean sink or large bowl with ice water. Fill a pot with water and place over medium high heat. Bring to a boil. Add clean dandelion leaves and cook for 1 minute. Immediately drain and place in the ice water. Once the leaves are completely cool, pat them dry. Place in freezer bags. Freeze for up to 1 year and use in recipes where the leaves are cooked.

Dehydrating: Place washed and dried dandelion leaves on the tray of a dehydrator. Set at 135 degrees F. and dehydrate until completely dry and crisp. Alternatively, place leaves on a wire cooling rack placed on top of a rimmed baking tray. Place in the oven at its lowest temperature setting until the leaves are completely dry. Allow the leaves to cool completely. Store in an air tight container in a cool, dry, dark location. Dehydrated dandelion leaves are perfect for soups and stews, or for crushing fine and using as a seasoning.

Canning: If you like canned spinach or collards, you will probably like canned dandelion leaves. First, be sure you are completely familiar with safe pressure canning guidelines. (You can find guidelines on my blog: http://proverbsthirtyonewoman. blogspot.com/2010/06/how-to-can-canning-beets.html#.UfwOuG1N6UY)

You will need about 28 lbs. of leaves to make 7 canned quarts. Wash a handful of leaves at a time, drain, and pat dry. Fill a pot with a steamer insert with a few inches of water. Place the leaves in the steamer and steam 3 to 5 minutes, or until completely wilted. If desired, add ½ teaspoon of salt to each canning jar. Fill each jar loosely with the leaves and pour fresh boiling water over them. Leave 1 inch headspace. Process pints for 70 minutes and quarts for 90 minutes.

When a Recipe Calls for Cooked Leaves...

...you may either:

* Bring a pot of water to a boil, boil the leaves for 1 minute (or until tender), drain, and place in ice water until completely cool.

* Place freshly washed, damp leaves in a skillet with a snug-fitting lid or in a pot with a steamer insert. Cook until limp and just tender. Drain.

* Sauté the leaves in a little oil until bright green and wilted.

> **If using larger dandelion leaves with thick stems, be sure to cut out the stems and discard them.**

Easy Dandelion Sauté

If dandelion leaves are new to you, this is a simple and easy first recipe to try. If you enjoy sautéed spinach, kale, and other greens, I think you'll find sautéed dandelion leaves please you, too.

1/4 teaspoon coarse salt
1 tablespoon olive oil
4 garlic cloves, minced
1 1/2 lbs. dandelion leaves, chopped coarsely
Pepper

1. In a small bowl, combine the garlic and salt.

2. Place a skillet over medium high heat and add the oil. Once warmed, add the garlic mixture, sautéing until the garlic barely starts turning color.

3. Add the dandelion leaves and season with pepper. Cook and stir often until the leaves are bright green and wilted.

Serves 2.

Variation: Cook a few strips of bacon in the skillet; drain on paper towels. Add the garlic and salt mixture, then the leaves. When the leaves are wilted, remove from the stove and crumble the bacon on top.

Spiced Dandelion Leaves

1/4 cup olive oil
2 garlic cloves, minced
2 lbs. dandelion leaves
1/2 teaspoon hot red pepper flakes
1/2 teaspoon salt

1. In a skillet placed over medium high heat, pour the oil. Once warmed, add the garlic, sautéing 30 seconds.

2. Add the dandelion leaves, red pepper flakes, and salt. Sauté until the liquid from the leaves has evaporated.

Serves 2 – 3.

Dandelion Noodles

If you love spinach noodles, you'll likely enjoy dandelion leaf noodles, too. Eat them simply, with a little butter and freshly grated Parmesan cheese, or try them with your favorite pasta sauce.

1 1/4 cups dandelion leaves
2 tablespoons water
1 egg
Salt
1 ¼ + cups all purpose flour

1. Place the dandelion leaves and water in a saucepan. Cover and cook until the leaves are tender. Allow to cool for several minutes.

2. Add the egg and a pinch or two of salt.

3. Using an immersion blender or a traditional blender, puree the mixture.

4. Pour the leaf mixture into a large mixing bowl and stir in 1 cup of flour. If the dough is still soft, add a little more flour and mix again, repeating until the dough is stiff.

5. Turn out the dough on a lightly floured surface, such as the counter. Knead for about 1 minute.

6. With the rolling pin, roll the dough very thin. Leave the dough as is for 20 minutes.

7. Loosely roll the dough. Use a sharp knife to cut strips ¼ inch wide. Unroll and cut into noodles of whatever length you desire.

8. You may now cook the noodles, or you may dry them for storage. To dry the noodles, leave them in a single layer on the lightly floured counter, place them in a food dehydrator, or hang them on a pasta drying rack or a clothes drying rack. To avoid spoilage, be sure the noodles are *completely* dry before storing them.

Serves 2 - 4.

Dandelion Leaf Vinegar

Splash this vinegar onto green salads, into cooked green and stir frys, in drinking water, or use in any way you'd use ordinary vinegar.

Fresh dandelion leaves
Raw, organic apple cider vinegar

1. Pack a glass jar with a plastic lid* tight with dandelion leaves.

2. Pour room temperature apple cider vinegar over the leaves until it comes nearly to the top of the jar. Place the jar in a dark location, like the pantry, for 6 to 8 weeks.

3. Strain through a fine sieve. (If desired, you may eat the "pickled" leaves.) Place in a clean jar with a plastic lid.*

* Vinegar reacts negatively with metal, so it's important to use a plastic lid.

Old Timey Dandelion Salad

2 – 4 bacon slices
½ cup apple cider vinegar
½ cup granulated sugar
About 1 large handful dandelion leaves

1. Place a skillet over medium high heat and cook the bacon. Drain on paper towels.

2. To the bacon drippings in the skillet, add the vinegar, sugar, and ½ cup water. Stir and cook until the sugar completely dissolves.

3. Place the dandelion leaves in a serving bowl. Crumble the bacon and add it to the bowl. Pour in the vinegar mixture and toss well.

Serves 2 – 4.

Tips for Cooking Bacon

For helpful tips on cooking bacon, see my blog:
http://goo.gl/jd6ag

Chicken and Dandelion Greens Stew

Instead of using spinach in your soups and stews, dandelion leaves are an excellent, nutritious, and free substitute.

2 tablespoons + 2 teaspoons olive oil
4 chicken breasts
Pepper
Salt
¼ cup all purpose flour
4 garlic cloves, chopped
2 cups packed dandelion leaves
14.5 oz. canned diced tomatoes (undrained)
14.5 oz. chicken or beef stock
1 tablespoon red wine vinegar
¼ teaspoon red pepper flakes (optional)
Freshly grated Parmesan cheese (optional)

1. Preheat the oven to 325 degrees F.

2. In a bowl, mix the flour with some salt and pepper.

3. Place a Dutch oven over medium-high heat. Add 2 tablespoons oil.

4. Dredge the chicken in the flour mixture. Working in batches, brown the chicken for about 1 ½ minutes on each side. Remove from the Dutch oven. Allow to cook a little, then shred with two forks.

5. Add 2 teaspoons oil. When the oil is warm, sauté the garlic for about 20 seconds. Add the dandelion leaves and cook until wilted.

6. Add the tomatoes and stock. Bring to a boil and return the chicken pieces to the Dutch oven. Cover and bake in the preheated oven for 1 hour and 15 minutes. Stir in the vinegar.

Serves 4 - 6.

DIY Stock or Broth

The best stock or broth is homemade. Homemade stock is low in sodium (unlike most store bought brands) and has better flavor, too. It's also easy to make. Learn how to make your own stock here: http://goo.gl/gJWO1

Pasta with Dandelion Leaf Sauce

Pasta with leafy greens such as spinach are fairly well known, but dandelion leaves work just as well.

5 cups penne pasta
Salt
2 lbs. dandelion leaves
1 tablespoon butter
1 onion, chopped
1 cup milk
1 tablespoon all purpose flour

Olive oil
Parmesan cheese
Pepper
Nutmeg

1. Fill a pot with water and a pinch or two of salt, and bring to a boil. Add the pasta and cook until tender. Drain, reserving the liquid. Fill a clean sink or large bowl with ice water.

2. Place the pasta-cooking liquid back in the pot and bring to a boil. Add the dandelion leaves and cook for 1 minute. Drain and place the leaves in the prepared ice water.

3. In a skillet placed over medium high heat, melt the butter. Add the onion and cook until tender and transparent.

4. Chop the dandelion leaves and add them to the skillet.

5. In a bowl, stir together the flour and milk. Reduce the heat and pour over the dandelion leaf mixture. Season with salt and pepper. Stir until the sauce is smooth and creamy.

6. Pour the pasta into a serving bowl and stir in the dandelion leaf mixture. Sprinkle with Parmesan cheese.

Serves 4 – 8.

Variation: Serve with cooked and crumbled bacon on top.

Dandelion Leaf and Potato Stew

3 tablespoons olive oil
2 cups diced onion
Salt
1 sweet potato, cut into 2 inch pieces
1 yellow potato, cut into 2 inch pieces
1/2 bell pepper, diced
4 cloves garlic, minced
1 tablespoon shredded fresh ginger

1 teaspoon ground coriander
1/2 teaspoon turmeric
1/4 teaspoon cayenne pepper
13 oz. coconut milk
2 cups chopped dandelion leaves

1. In a large pot placed over medium high heat, warm the olive oil. Add the onion and salt, sautéing until softened.

2. Add the potatoes, bell pepper, garlic, ginger, coriander, turmeric, and cayenne pepper. Sauté for 1 minute.

3. Add the coconut milk and dandelion leaves. Bring to a boil. Reduce heat, cover, and gently simmer until potatoes are tender, about 20 to 25 minutes.

Serves 4 – 6.

Dandelion Egg Salad

4 eggs, hardboiled and chopped
¾ cup chopped dandelion greens
1 teaspoon horseradish
1 tablespoon chopped fresh chives
½ cup mayonnaise

1. Fill a pot with water and bring to a boil. Fill a clean sink or large bowl with ice water.

2. Once the water boils, add the dandelion leaves and cook for exactly 1 minute. Immediately drain and place the leaves in the ice water.

3. When the leaves are completely cool, drain them and place in a large bowl.

4. Add the chives, horseradish, eggs, and mayonnaise, and mix well.

Serves 2.

Dandelion and Chicken Casserole

1 lb. dandelion leaves, cooked
8 oz. skinless boneless chicken breasts, cubed into ½ inch pieces
2 tablespoons butter
1 tablespoon all purpose flour
3/4 cup heavy whipping cream
1/4 cup chicken stock
1/8 teaspoon ground nutmeg
2 eggs
3/4 cup breadcrumbs
1 tablespoon olive oil
Salt
Pepper

1. Preheat the oven to 400 degrees F. Butter a 9 inch pie plate and set aside. Season the chicken with salt and pepper.

2. In a skillet placed over medium high heat, melt 1 tablespoon of butter. Add the chicken and cook until golden. Remove from the skillet and transfer to a bowl.

3. Add the remaining butter to the skillet and allow it to melt. Add the flour and whisk for 30 seconds. Add the cream and bring to a boil, whisking constantly, until thickened and smooth.

4. Whisk in the stock. Add the dandelion leaves. Add the nutmeg; season with salt and pepper.

5. Add the eggs and mix well, being sure to break the yolks. Spread the mixture in the prepared pie plate. Sprinkle the chicken on top, and press down with a spatula. Sprinkle with breadcrumbs and drizzle with oil.

6. Bake for about 19 minutes, or until golden and eggs thoroughly cooked.

Serves 4 – 8.

Adapted from a recipe that appeared in the May 2009 issue of Bon Appétit.

Dandelion and Mushroom Pasta

1 lb. pasta
3 cups dandelion leaves
1 tablespoon + olive oil
6 garlic cloves
8 oz. sliced mushrooms
14 oz. chicken stock
Pepper
1 teaspoon fresh thyme
Romano cheese

1. Fill a large pot with water and place it over medium high heat. Bring to a boil. Add the pasta and cook until tender. Drain, reserving the water.

2. Fill a clean sink or large bowl with ice water. Pour the reserved cooking water back into the pot and place over medium high heat.

3. When the water comes to a boil, add the dandelion leaves and cook for 1 minute. Drain and immediately place in the ice water.

4. Place a skillet over medium high heat and add a tablespoon of olive oil. Once warmed, add the garlic and sauté for 30 seconds. Add the mushrooms, adding additional oil, if needed. Sauté for 5 minutes.

5. Add the stock, dandelion leaves, thyme, and a little pepper to taste.

6. Pour the pasta into a bowl and add the leaf mixture, tossing well. Sprinkle with cheese.

Serves 4 - 8.

Dandelion Chips with Balsamic Vinegar

If you enjoy kale chips, give dandelion chips a try. In this recipe, the balsamic vinegar is a nice complement the slight bitterness of the leaves.

¾ - 1 lb. dandelion leaves
1/8 cup melted coconut oil or olive oil
1/8 cup balsamic vinegar
1/4 teaspoon garlic powder
About 1/4 teaspoon salt
About 1/4 teaspoon pepper

1. Preheat the oven to 325 degrees F. Line baking sheets with parchment paper; set aside.* Cut the dandelion leaves into the size of your choice – usually about the size of a potato chip. Or, leave them whole.

2. In a bowl, mix together the oil, vinegar, garlic powder, and salt. Toss the leaves into this mixture.

3. Lay the leaves in a single layer on the baking sheets. Drizzle the remaining oil mixture over the leaves. Bake for 12-16 minutes, watching carefully to ensure the chips don't burn. The leaves will harden as they cool.

* If desired, you may make dandelion chips in a food dehydrator set at 135 degrees F.

Dandelion Chips with Sea Salt

Dandelion leaves
Olive oil
Sea salt

1. Preheat the oven to 325 degrees F. Line baking sheets with parchment paper; set aside.* Cut the dandelion leaves into the size of your choice – usually about the size of a potato chip. Or, leave them whole.

3. Drizzle the leaves lightly with olive oil. They should be well coated by oil, but not soggy. Lay the leaves in a single layer on the baking sheets.

4. Bake for 12-16 minutes, watching carefully to ensure the chips don't burn.

5. Season with sea salt. The leaves will harden as they cool.

* If desired, you may make dandelion chips in a food dehydrator set at 135 degrees F.

Spicy Dandelion Chips

Dandelion leaves
Olive oil
Salt
Chile flakes
Paprika

1. Preheat the oven to 325 degrees F. Line baking sheets with parchment paper; set aside.* Cut the dandelion leaves into the size of

your choice – usually about the size of a potato chip. Or, leave them whole.

3. Drizzle olive oil lightly over the leaves and toss until well coated, but not soggy. Add salt and chile flakes and toss again. Lay the leaves in a single layer on the baking sheets.

4. Bake for 12-16 minutes, watching carefully to ensure the chips don't burn.

5. Season with paprika. The leaves will harden as they cool.

* If desired, you may make dandelion chips in a food dehydrator set at 135 degrees F.

Beans with Dandelion Greens

1 lb. dried great northern beans
1 onion, minced
1 carrot, chopped
2 garlic cloves, minced
1/2 teaspoon dried thyme
1/2 teaspoon dried marjoram
1 1/2 cups chopped leaves
2 tablespoons butter
Salt
Pepper

1. Pour the dry beans in a pot and cover with 3 to 4 inches of warm water. Place a kitchen towel over the pot and allow the beans to soak for at least 4 hours. Drain.

2. Pour the beans into a Dutch oven. Add the onion, carrot, garlic, thyme, and marjoram; mix well. Add enough water to cover the whole by 1 inch. Cover.

3. Place the Dutch oven on the stove over medium high heat. Bring to a boil. Reduce the heat and simmer for an hour, adding more water, if needed, to keep the beans covered.

4. Add the dandelion leaves and keep cooking for another half hour, or until the beans are tender.

5. Remove the Dutch oven from the stove and add the butter, stirring in until melted. Season with salt and pepper.

Serves 4 – 8.

Pasta with Tomatoes and Dandelion Greens

1 lb. dandelion greens, chopped into ½ inch pieces and cooked
2 oz. pancetta (or 3 - 4 strips bacon), diced
1 medium onion, chopped
2 garlic cloves, minced
1/8 teaspoon crushed red pepper flakes
28 oz. can diced tomatoes (undrained)
1/4 cup water
8 oz. pasta shells (about 3 cups)
Salt
Pepper
1/2 cup freshly grated Parmesan cheese

1. In a skillet placed over medium high heat, cook the pancetta or bacon until just cooked through. Drain on paper towels. Pour off all but 2 teaspoons of the pan drippings.

2. Add the onion to the skillet. Sauté until tender.

3. Add the garlic and red pepper flakes and cook for another 60 seconds. Add the pancetta or bacon, the tomatoes (including the liquid in the can), and the water. Bring to a simmer. Cook until thickened, about 20 minutes.

4. In the meantime, fill a large pot with salted water and bring to a boil. Add the pasta and cook until tender. Reserve ¼ cup of the pasta water and drain off the rest.

5. To the tomato mixture, add the cooked pasta, the leaves, and the reserved pasta water. Cook and stir for 1 minute. Season with salt and pepper.

6. Ladle into individual bowls and sprinkle with cheese before serving.

Serves 4 – 6.

Adapted from a recipe from the Winter 2003 issue of Eating Well.

Artichoke Hearts and Dandelion Salad

3/4 lb. dandelion leaves, chopped
3 cups chopped romaine leaves
1 bunch mild radishes, sliced thin
12 oz. marinated artichoke hearts
1 tablespoons red wine vinegar
Salt
¼ teaspoon Dijon mustard
1 garlic clove, minced

1. In a serving bowl, combine the dandelion leaves and romaine.

2. Drain the liquid from the artichoke hearts into a small bowl. Add the vinegar, a pinch of salt, mustard, and garlic; mix well.

3. Pour the vinegar dressing over the greens and toss well. Sprinkle the artichoke hearts on top of the salad.

Serves 4 – 6.

Adapted from a recipe at Frugal-Café.com.

Scalloped Dandelions

2 tablespoons bacon drippings
2 tablespoons all purpose flour
3/4 cup water
2 cups milk
Salt

1 tablespoon vinegar
2 teaspoons granulated sugar
1 cup chopped dandelion leaves
1/4 cup minced onion
2 eggs, hardboiled and sliced

1. Add the bacon drippings to a skillet placed over medium high heat. Once melted, add the flour and whisk until well combined.

2. Add the water, milk, a pinch of salt, vinegar, and sugar, mixing well and stirring until the sugar dissolves.

3. Add the dandelion leaves and the onion. Remove from the stove immediately. Add the eggs.

Serves 4 - 6.

Based upon a recipe at Cooks.com.

Dandelion Leaves, Beans, and Eggs

3 tablespoons+ olive oil
4 cloves garlic, sliced thin (divided)
8 cups chopped dandelion leaves
Salt
Pepper
1 cup chopped onion
1 teaspoon cumin seeds
1/4 teaspoon paprika
15 oz. garbanzo beans, drained
5 canned whole tomatoes, crushed
3 cups+ beef, chicken, or vegetable stock
4 eggs

1. In a pot placed over medium heat, warm 1 tablespoon oil. Add the slices from 1 clove garlic; sauté until golden.

2. Add the dandelion leaves, tossing to coat with oil. Season with salt and pepper. Cook until just wilted. Transfer the leaves and garlic to a bowl and set aside.

3. Add 2 tablespoons oil to the pot. Add the onion and the remaining garlic slices. Sauté until the onion is soft.

4. Add the cumin and paprika. Sauté for 1 minute. Stir in the beans and tomatoes. Cook until the beans begin browning, about 8 to 10 minutes.

5. Add stock. Bring to a simmer, scraping the bottom of the pan with a spoon. Reduce the heat and simmer until thickened, about 15 to 20 minutes.

6. During this simmering, mash some of the garbanzo beans with the back of a spoon.

7. Fold in the leaves and simmer for another 8 to 10 minutes. If the liquid nearly evaporates, add more stock.

8. In the meantime, place a heavy skillet over medium high heat and add enough oil to reach a depth of 1/8 inch. Once hot, crack 2 eggs into the oil. Use a spoon to gently baste the whites of the eggs with oil. Cook until the whites are golden and crunchy, about 2 to 3 minutes. Do not turn the eggs. Season eggs with salt and pepper. Transfer to a plate and repeat with remaining eggs.

8. To serve, ladle the garbanzo bean mixture into bowls and top each one with an egg.

Serves 4 – 6.

Dandelion Quiche

Pastry for 9 inch pie (single crust)
6 slices bacon, chopped (or ½ cup cooked, cubed ham)
5 cups chopped dandelion leaves
5 cups fresh baby spinach leaves (or torn full-sized spinach leaves)
3 green onions (scallions), sliced thin
½ cup shredded Swiss cheese
1 egg, white and yolk divided
3 eggs (whole)
½ cup shredded Swiss or Jarlsberg cheese
1 cup heavy whipping cream
¾ cup milk
Salt
¼ teaspoon dry basil
1/8 teaspoon ground nutmeg
Pepper

1. Preheat the oven to 375 degrees F. Lay the pastry into a 9 inch pie plate and line with two layers of foil. Add pie weights, uncooked rice, or dried beans to the bottom and bake, according to the pastry recipe.

2. Three minutes before the pastry is done, remove the foil and weights. When pastry is done baking, cool in pie plate on a wire rack.

3. In a skillet placed over medium high heat, cook the bacon. Drain on paper towels. Reserve 1 tablespoon of the bacon drippings in the skillet.

4. Add the dandelion greens, spinach, and green onions. Sauté until the greens are wilted.

5. Brush the quiche crust with the egg white.

6. In the bottom of the crust, lay the cooked greens. Follow with a layer of the cheese, and end with the bacon.

7. In a large mixing bowl, whisk the cream, milk, a pinch of salt, basil, nutmeg, and a little pepper. Pour over the top of the quiche.

8. Bake for 35 – 40 minutes, or until a knife inserted in the center of the quiche comes out clean. Allow to stand 10 minutes before cutting or serving.

Serves 6.

Crockpot Gingered Dandelions, Chicken, and Chickpeas

1 tablespoon olive oil
1 large onion, chopped
4 garlic cloves, minced
2 tablespoons fresh, peeled, shredded ginger
2 1/2 teaspoons ground coriander
Salt
Pepper
2 teaspoons balsamic vinegar
28 oz. chopped tomatoes
30 oz. chickpeas (garbanzo beans), drained
4 boneless, skinless chicken breasts
2 cups dandelion leaves, cooked

1. Pour the olive oil into a large skillet and place over medium heat. Add the onions and sauté until transparent.

2. Add the garlic and ginger and sauté for 30 seconds. Add the coriander. Add some salt and pepper. Sauté for about 1 minute. Stir in the vinegar and tomatoes. Bring to a boil.

3. Place the chicken in the crock pot. Pour the drained chickpeas over it. Pour the onion mixture and stir. Cover and cook on low for 6 to 8 hours or on high for 3 to 4 hours.

4. Shred the chicken with two forks and stir back into the mixture. Stir in the dandelion greens.

Serves 2 – 4.

Red Potato and Dandelion Leaf Salad

1 lb. red potatoes
1 large bunch of dandelion leaves (about a large handful), coarsely chopped
1 head Belgian endive (a.k.a. chicory; or radicchio), coarsely chopped
3 tablespoons olive oil
2 garlic cloves, minced
1 can white kidney beans, drained
Juice and zest (grated peel) of 1 lemon
2 tablespoons ricotta cheese
Salt
Pepper

1. Fill a pot with water and place over medium high heat. Bring to a boil and add the potatoes. Cook until tender. Drain and allow to cool slightly before cutting potatoes in half.

2. In a skillet placed over medium high heat, add the oil. Once warmed, add the garlic, sautéing for 30 seconds. Add the dandelion leaves and endive, sautéing until wilted. Season with salt and pepper.

3. Add the beans and the potatoes; toss.

4. Add the lemon juice and zest. Add the ricotta; toss well. Serve warm or cold.

Serves 6 – 8.

Adapted from a recipe at StraightFromTheFarm.net.

Dandelion and Lima Bean Soup

1 cup dried lima beans
2 bunches dandelion leaves, coarsely chopped
3 tablespoons olive oil
2 stalks celery stalks, finely chopped
2 carrots, finely chopped
1 onion, finely chopped
8 cups chicken stock
14 ½ oz. diced tomatoes, drained
1/2 cup freshly grated Parmesan cheese

1. Pour the beans into a large pot and add enough cold water to cover by 3 inches; allow to soak overnight. Drain.

2. Pour the beans back into the pot and add enough fresh water to cover by 2 inches. Place over medium high heat and bring to a boil. Reduce the heat and simmer until beans are tender, about 45 minutes.

3. Add the dandelion leaves. Cook 5 minutes. Drain.

4. In the same pot, pour 3 tablespoons of oil and place over medium high heat. Once warmed, add the celery, carrots, and onion. Sauté until onion is translucent

5. Add the stock, tomatoes, and bean mixture. Reduce heat to low and simmer 20 minutes.

6. Remove from the heat and cover. Allow to sit 15 minutes before serving. When serving, sprinkle cheese over each bowl.

Serves 4 – 8.

Dandelion and Sausage Risotto

This familiar-looking rice dish is another ideal introduction to dandelion leaves. The dandelions add great flavor, but look little different from spinach or kale mixed into the rice.

4 tablespoons butter, divided
1 small onion, chopped
1 garlic clove, minced
6 oz. mild Italian sausage, casings removed
2 cups arborio rice
1 cup dry white wine
5 cups chicken stock
1 bunch (about 1 large handful) dandelion leaves, cooked and chopped into ¾ inch pieces
3/4 cup (packed) freshly grated Parmesan cheese
Salt
Pepper

1. In a saucepan placed over medium high heat, melt 1 tablespoon butter. Add the onion and garlic and sauté until the onion is translucent.

2. Add the sausage and sauté until cooked through, breaking up chunks with a spoon.

3. Add the rice and stir for 1 minute.

4. Add the wine and reduce the heat to medium-low. Simmer until the wine is almost completely absorbed.

5. Add 1 cup of stock and stir until it is almost completely absorbed.

6. Add the remaining 4 cups of stock, 1/2 cup at a time, letting it absorb into the mixture before adding more.

7. Add the dandelion leaves. Cook until the rice is tender and the mixture is creamy, about 25 minutes total.

8. Add the cheese and remaining 3 tablespoons butter. Season with salt and pepper.

Serves 4 – 6.

Adapted from a recipe in the May 2009 issue of Bon Appétit.

Dandelion and Asparagus Risotto

1 tablespoon olive oil
1 cup chopped onion
1 cup arborio rice
4 oz. dandelion leaves
3 cups chicken stock
Salt
Nutmeg
1/2 cup freshly grated Parmesan cheese
1 1/2 cups asparagus, chopped into 1 inch pieces

1. Preheat the oven to 400 degrees F.

2. Place a Dutch oven over medium heat and add the oil. Once warmed, add the onions and sauté until tender.

3. Add the rice, stirring until coated with the oil and onion mixture.

4. Add the dandelion leaves, a pinch of salt, a pinch of nutmeg, and 2 cups of stock. Bring to a simmer; cook for 7 minutes.

5. Stir in 1/4 cup of the cheese. Remove from the stove, cover, and bake for 15 minutes.

6. Stir in the asparagus and the remaining 1/4 cup of cheese. If the mixture seems dry, add a little stock (up to 1 cup).

7. Cover and bake another 15 minutes, or until the liquid is nearly absorbed.

Serves 4 – 6.

Dandelion Leaf, Leek, and Potato Soup

1 tablespoon olive oil
6 oz. pork sausage
2 leeks, white and light green parts only, chopped
4 garlic cloves, sliced thin
Salt
1 cup dry white wine or chicken stock
1 lb. potatoes, sliced thin
4 cups chicken or beef stock
8 cups chopped spinach
1 bunch green onions (scallions), sliced
15 oz. cannellini or Great Northern beans, drained
1/4 cup chopped fresh chives (optional)
¼ cup chopped fresh parsley leaves (optional)

1. In a large pot placed over medium heat, warm the oil. Add the sausage and leeks. Cook, crumbling the sausage and stirring occasionally, until the leeks are tender, about 5 minutes.

2. Add the garlic and salt. Cook and stir for about 20 seconds. Add the wine. Cover and bring to a boil over high heat.

3. Uncover and cook until the wine is nearly evaporated, about 4 minutes.

4. Add the potatoes and stock. Cover and bring to a boil.

5. Stir in the dandelion leaves and green onions. Cover and cook until the potatoes are tender, about 5 minutes.

6. Remove from the stove and stir in the beans. Cover and allow to stand for 1 minute.

7. When serving, sprinkle chives and parsley over each individual bowl, if desired.

Serves 4 – 6.

Dandelion Greens with Camembert Toast

In the South, greens of all types – including dandelion leaves - are commonly eaten with eggs. This meal is simple, but hearty enough to serve any time of the day.

1 tablespoon butter, room temperature
4 (½ inch thick) baguette slices
1 tablespoon white wine vinegar
1 1/2 tablespoons minced shallot
1 teaspoon Dijon mustard
3 tablespoons olive oil
4 oz. Camembert cheese, cut into 4 equal pieces
5 cups chopped dandelion leaves

1. Toast the baguette slices. If they won't fit in your toaster, place them on top of a wire cooling rack placed atop a rimmed baking sheet; place in a preheated 450 degree F. oven for 5 minutes, or until golden. Butter immediately.

2. Preheat the oven's broiler.

3. In a mixing bowl, stir together the vinegar, shallot, and mustard. Little by little, stir in the oil, blending well.

4. On top of each piece of toast, place a piece of cheese. Place the toast on a rimmed baking sheet and broil 4 inches from the heat until the cheese begins melting.

5. Toss the dandelion leaves into the vinegar mixture.

6. Serve the dandelion leaf mixture with the toast on the side.

Serves 2 – 4.

Dandelion Greens with Hot Olive Oil Dressing

1/4 cup olive oil
3 garlic cloves, sliced thin

1/3 cup sliced almonds
1/2 cup golden raisins
2 tablespoons Sherry vinegar
1/2 teaspoon granulated sugar
Salt
Pepper
1 lb. dandelion leaves

1. Place the dandelion leaves in a serving bowl.

2. In a skillet placed over medium high heat, add the oil. Once warmed, add the garlic and almonds, stirring often, until the nuts are golden.

3. Add the raisins and sauté until they look plump, about 1 minute. Remove the skillet from the stove.

4. Stir in the vinegar and sugar. Season with salt and pepper. Pour the mixture over the dandelion leaves. Toss.

Serves 2.

Adapted from a recipe in the April 2007 issue of Gourmet.

Dandelion and Cumin Cornbread

Dandelion leaves and Southern food (like cornbread) have gone hand in hand for generations. This recipe gives a nod to the Southwest and is ideal for serving with Mexican or Southwestern food.

1 tablespoon olive oil
4 cups chopped dandelion leaves
1 teaspoon whole cumin seeds
½ teaspoon red pepper flakes
Juice from 1 lemon
1 cup all purpose flour
1 cup cornmeal
2 teaspoons baking powder
½ teaspoon baking soda
¼ cup sugar
1 teaspoon salt
1⅓ cups milk
4 tablespoons butter, melted
2 eggs
1 cup frozen or fresh corn kernels
Olive oil spray

1. Preheat the oven to 375 degrees F. Place a 9 inch cast iron skillet or 9 x 9 inch metal baking pan in the oven to preheat.

2. Pour the oil into another skillet, placed over medium high heat. Once the oil is warm, add the dandelion leaves, cumin, and red pepper flakes. Sauté about 10 minutes, or until the liquid has evaporated and the leaves are tender.

3. Drizzle the leaves with lemon juice and toss to combine.

4. In a large mixing bowl, stir together the flour, cornmeal, baking powder, baking soda, sugar, and salt.

5. In another bowl, whisk the milk, butter, and eggs together. Stir the milk mixture into the flour mixture, until just blended.

6. Fold in the dandelion leaves and corn.

7. Remove the pre-heated skillet from the oven; lightly spray with oil.

8. Pour the batter into the prepared skillet and bake for 30 - 35 minutes, or until golden. Remove the skillet to a wire cooling rack and allow the bread to cool in the pan.

Serves 8.

Dandelion Pizza

For the Dough:
4 ½ teaspoons active dry yeast
2 tablespoons granulated sugar
1/4 cup + olive oil
2 teaspoons coarse salt
4 cups + all purpose flour

Topping:
1 tablespoon olive oil
1 garlic clove, minced
1 ½ cups dandelion leaves, cooked
1 cup shredded mozzarella cheese
2 plum or cherry tomatoes, sliced thin
4 oz. feta cheese with garlic & herb, crumbled (optional)
1 teaspoon chopped fresh rosemary
Freshly grated Parmesan cheese

1. Make the crust: Pour 1 1/2 cups warm water into a large mixing bowl; add the yeast. Allow to stand until foamy, about 5 minutes.

2. Add the sugar, oil, and salt; stir. Stir in the flour. The dough will be sticky. Cover the bowl with plastic wrap and place in a warm location until doubled, about 60 minutes. In the meantime, preheat the oven to 450 degrees F.

3. Lightly flour a counter or other work surface. Turn out the dough onto the counter and knead once or twice. Divide the dough in half. Freeze one half for future use. Place the other half onto a pizza pan and press with your hands to shape.

4. Combine garlic and oil in a small saucepan and heat over medium high until warmed, but not hot. (Or, place the garlic and oil in a small, microwavable bowl and microwave for 30 seconds.)

5. Spread the dandelion leaves, mozzarella cheese, tomato slices, and feta (if using) on top of the pizza crust. Sprinkle rosemary and Parmesan on top.

6. Bake until the cheese is melted and the crust is golden, about 10 - 12 minutes. Allow to stand 5 – 10 minutes before cutting or serving.

Serves 4.

Savory Dandelion Clafoutis

A clafoutis is an open-faced French dessert, usually made with fruit (like cherries). This dish, however, is savory, not sweet – something like a quiche.

7 oz. dandelion leaves, coarsely chopped
3.5 oz. ricotta cheese (weighed after straining through cheesecloth)
1 green onion (scallion), minced
2 eggs
3 tablespoons freshly grated Parmesan cheese
3 tablespoons olive oil
Salt
Pepper

1. Preheat the oven to 350 degrees F. Butter individual-sized baking dishes, or one larger baking dish; set aside.

2. Pour the oil into a skillet over medium high heat. Once warmed, add the onion and sauté until tender.

3. Add the dandelion leaves and sauté for an additional 2 minutes. Remove from the stove and pour the leaf mixture into a bowl to allow to cool completely.

4. In another bowl, whisk together the ricotta and eggs. Stir in the Parmesan. Season with salt and pepper.

5. Once the leaf mixture is completely cool, fold into the ricotta mixture. Pour the mixture into the prepared baking dishes. Place the baking dishes on a rimmed baking sheet.

6. Bake for approximately 10 minutes, or until risen and golden.

Serves 4 – 6.

Adapted from a recipe at undejeunerdesoleil.com.

Dandelion Bread Pudding

1 bunch (about a large handful) dandelion leaves, chopped
1 onion, minced
2 garlic cloves, minced
1/4 cup dried tomatoes, chopped
1 teaspoon red pepper flakes
2 eggs
1 1/4 cup heavy cream
1 cup grated Gruyere cheese
3 cups toasted and cubed bread
Salt
Pepper

1. Preheat the oven to 350 degrees F.

2. Pour the oil into a large skillet placed over medium high heat. Once warmed, add the onion, garlic, red pepper flakes, and dried tomatoes. Sauté until tender.

3. Add the dandelion leaves and season with salt and pepper. Sauté until the leaves are wilted. Remove from the heat.

4. In a large mixing bowl, whisk together the eggs, cream, and cheese. Stir in the bread. Allow the bread to soak for about 5 minutes.

5. Fold the leaf mixture into the bread mixture.

6. Pour the mixture into a 9 x 13 inch baking dish. Bake for 45 – 60 minutes, or until no longer runny.

Serves 4 – 6.

Variation: Sprinkle additional cheese on top before baking.

Pumpkin-Dandelion Soup

1 small sugar pumpkin
1 onion, chopped
6 garlic cloves, minced
2 tablespoons butter
6 cups water
1 large handful dandelion leaves, cooked and chopped into bite-sized pieces
1 cup heavy cream
½ teaspoon nutmeg
Salt

1. Preheat the oven to 350 degrees F.

2. Place the whole pumpkin on a rimmed baking sheet and bake for about 60 minutes, or until a fork easily pierces the rind. Allow to

cool slightly, then cut in half and scoop out the seeds and stringy parts; discard. Peel off the rind.

3. With a potato masher, blender, or food processor, puree the "meat" of the pumpkin and measure out 4 cups. (Any remaining pumpkin puree can be frozen for future use.)

4. Place a large pot over medium high heat and add the butter. Once melted, add the onion and garlic and sauté until the onion is tender.

5. Add the water, dandelion leaves, and pureed pumpkin. Season with a pinch or two of salt. Simmer for 30 minutes.

6. Add the heavy cream and nutmeg and cook for another few minutes.

Serves 6 – 12.

Dandelion-Horseradish Egg Salad

4 eggs, hardboiled and chopped
2/3 cup cooked and chopped dandelion leaves
1 teaspoon horseradish
1 tablespoon chopped fresh chives
½ cup mayonnaise

1. In a serving bowl, stir together the eggs, dandelion leaves, chives, and horseradish. Stir in the mayonnaise.

Serves 2.

Salmon with Dandelions, Lentils, and Bacon

Dandelion leaves are fantastic served alongside, on top of, or under any type of meat, poultry, or fish.

1 1/2 – 2 lbs. of salmon fillets
Salt
2 slices bacon, cut in half

1/4 cup finely chopped carrots
1/2 cup chopped onion
1/2 lb. lentils
2 1/2 cups water
1 1/2 tablespoons red wine vinegar
Pepper
1 cup chopped dandelion leaves
2 teaspoons olive oil
Salt
Parsley, chopped

1. Season the salmon fillets with salt and place skin side up on a plate.

2. Place a skillet over medium high heat and add the bacon. Cook until nearly done.

3. Add the carrots and cook for about 5 minutes, or until they begin softening. Add the onion and cook until translucent.

4. Stir in the lentils. Stir in the water and bring to a simmer. Season with a pinch or two of salt. Cover and cook about 40 minutes, or until the lentils are tender. Not all of the liquid should evaporate. Add additional water, if needed, to maintain a slightly soup-like mixture.

5. Add the vinegar and season with pepper. Stir, then taste. If needed, add more salt, pepper, and/or vinegar. Aim for a slightly sour flavor.

6. Add the dandelion leaves and stir in. Reduce heat.

7. Place another skillet over high heat and add 1 tablespoon oil. When the oil sizzles when you flick a little water at it, add the salmon fillets, skin side down. (If necessary, work in batches.) Reduce heat to medium

8. Cook until fillets are nearly done, about 3 to 5 minutes. Remove the skillet from the stove, turn the fillets over, and finish cooking off the stove.

9. Pour 1/2 cup of the lentil mixture into shallow serving bowls. Place a salmon fillet in each, skin side up. Sprinkle with parsley.

Serves 4 – 6.

Adapted from a recipe in the July 7, 2011 edition of The Los Angeles Times.

Old Fashioned Dandelion Crowns

The first time you serve this dish, less adventurous eaters may be put off by an unfamiliar, sprawling dandelion crown on their plate. However, serving the whole crown allows for a combination of tasty leaves and the sweeter heart of the dandelion, which is similar in flavor to artichoke.

1 dandelion crown (the entire plant, root cut off, stems removed)
Salt
Pepper
1 tablespoon butter (optional)

1. Place the dandelion crown in a pot and add enough water to just cover. Bring to a boil, then reduce heat and simmer 5 minutes. Drain.

2. Taste. If the leaves aren't too bitter, go to step 3. Otherwise, place the crown back in the pot and repeat step 1 – but add a pinch or two of salt to the water.

3. After draining, add a dab of butter, if desired, tossing until the butter melts. Season with salt and pepper and serve.

Serves 1.

Variation: Omit step 3 and instead set the crown aside. In a bowl, combine 1/2 cup olive oil, ¼ cup apple cider or red wine vinegar, a little salt and pepper, 1 minced garlic clove, and 1 minced small onion. Add the crown and marinate for at least 4 hours.

Dandelion Stuffed Pork Loin

Here's another excellent introduction to eating dandelion leaves. While the recipe is a little more complicated than some of the others in this cookbook, it is not a difficult dish to pull off, and is suitable for company or for everyday meals.

3 ½ lbs. pork loin, butterflied
8 slices bacon
6 cups dandelion leaves
¼ cup onion, chopped
3 teaspoons olive oil
4 - 6 tablespoons dandelion wine (or white wine)
10 garlic cloves, roasted
1 ½ tablespoons fresh rosemary
¼ cup white raisins
1 cup breadcrumbs
Salt
Pepper

For the Sauce:
½ cup dandelion wine (or a dry white wine)
½ cup dry white wine
2 cups chicken stock
2 teaspoons corn starch
1 ½ teaspoons water
2 teaspoons butter

1. Preheat the oven to 450 degrees F.

2. Place a skillet over medium high heat and add the olive oil. Once warmed, add the onion, wine, and dandelion leaves. Cover and simmer until the leaves are tender. If the liquid cooks out before the leaves are tender, add more wine.

3. Strain. Pour the leaf mixture into a food processor or blender.

4. Add garlic, rosemary, raisins, and a little salt and pepper. Chop – *do not puree*. Pour mixture into a bowl

5. Add breadcrumbs, mixing well. Set aside.

6. Lay the pork flat, and place the bacon slices on top. Spoon the leaf mixture over on top of this. Roll the pork into a cylinder and close with toothpicks. Place in a roasting pan.

7. Roast in the preheated oven for 15 minutes. Reduce the heat to 325 degrees F. and roast until a thermometer reads 145 degrees F., about another 45 to 55 minutes.

8. Remove the pork from the roasting pan and cover loosely with foil. Allow to rest for 10 minutes.

9. In the meantime, make the sauce: To the roasting pan, add the wines and stock. Place over two of the stove's burners set to medium high heat. Stir, scraping the bottom of the pan. In a bowl, whisk the cornstarch and water. Add to the pan a little at a time, whisking each time. Add butter and whisk as it melts. Continue cooking until sauce is thickened.

10. To serve, slice the pork and spoon the sauce over each serving.

Serves 2 – 4.

Adapted from a recipe at Shine.Yahoo.com.

Dandelion and Potato Soup

4 cups water
1 stick of butter
6 cups chopped dandelion leaves
4 large potatoes, diced

2/3 cup cream
1 egg yolk
Salt
1 teaspoon lemon juice
Paprika

1. In a large saucepan placed over low heat, add the water, butter, and dandelion leaves. Bring to a boil.

2. Add the potatoes. Reduce heat, cover, and simmer for 35 minutes.

3. In a small bowl, whisk the egg yolk and cream together.

4. A little at a time, add the egg mixture to the soup. Add a little salt and the lemon juice.

5. Serve with a sprinkling of paprika on top.

Serves 4 to 6.

Adapted from a recipe in Peter A. Gail's Dandelion Celebration.

Dandelions and Ham

The sweetness of ham is well complimented by dandelion leaves.

1 ¼ cups dandelion leaves, cooked
1 teaspoon butter
½ lbs. ham, diced
1 garlic cloves, minced
¼ cup evaporated skim milk
¼ teaspoon Tabasco sauce

1. In a skillet placed over medium high heat, melt the butter. Add the ham and brown on every side. Transfer to a serving dish.

2. Add the garlic to the skillet and sauté for 30 seconds. Add the dandelion leaves and cook until wilted and slightly crisp. Stir in the Tabasco.

3. Spoon the leaf mixture over the ham.

Serves 1 – 2.

Dandelion Mashed Potato Casserole

1 lb. potatoes, peeled (if desired) and cut into quarters
Salt
1 lb. dandelion leaves
1/4 to 1/2 cup olive oil
Pepper
1 cup breadcrumbs

1. Place the potatoes in a large pot and cover with water. Place over medium high heat and bring to a boil. Boil until tender; drain, reserving the water.

2. In the meantime, fill a clean sink or bowl with ice water and preheat the oven to 400 degrees F.

3. Pour the water back into the pot and bring back to a boil. Add the dandelion leaves and cook 1 minute. Drain and place leaves in the ice water. Once cool, drain and chop.

4. Mash the potatoes with a potato masher or mixer, adding a little olive oil to make them moist. Mash the leaves, adding oil, if needed. Fold the leaves into the potatoes and season with salt and pepper.

3. Pour the potato mixture into a casserole dish and sprinkle with breadcrumbs. Drizzle with a little olive oil and season with salt and pepper. Bake about 15 minutes, or until breadcrumbs are golden.

Serves 4.

Cream of Dandelion Soup

6 cups dandelion leaves
1 tablespoon butter
2 leeks, white and light green parts only, sliced
1 carrot, diced
4 cups chicken stock
2 1/2 cups milk
1 tablespoon Dijon mustard
Salt
Pepper

1. Place the butter in a large pot placed over medium high heat. Once melted, add the dandelion leaves, carrot, and leeks. Sauté until tender.

2. Add the stock and simmer for 15 minutes.

3. Reduce the heat to medium. Whisk in the milk. Cook and stir often, until thickened. Remove from the stove and allow to cool slightly.

4. Using an immersion blender (or working in batches with a traditional blender), puree. Add the mustard and season with salt and pepper.

Serves 4.

Eggs, Toast, and Dandelion Greens

4 garlic cloves, chopped
1/4 teaspoon red pepper flakes (optional)
1 lb. dandelion greens, coarsely chopped
1/4 cup water
Salt
4 slices bread
2 to 4 eggs

1. Pour a little oil into a skillet placed over medium high heat. Once warmed, add the garlic and red pepper flakes (if using) and sauté for 20 seconds.

2. Add the dandelion leaves a handful at a time, until wilted and bright green.

3. Add the water and a pinch or two of salt. Cover and cook over medium low, stirring once in a while, until the leaves are tender. Add more water, if necessary, too prevent the mixture from going dry. Transfer to a bowl, cover, and set aside.

4. Lightly wipe out the skillet, adding a little oil if needed. Fry the eggs.

5. Toast the bread and place on serving plates. Top with the leaf mixture (including the liquid), then top with fried eggs.

Serves 2 – 4.

Chicken and Dandelion Soup

1 chicken (about 4 1/2 lbs.)
Salt
Pepper

1 lb. ground beef
1 egg
3 tablespoons chopped basil
1 teaspoon lemon zest (grated peel)
1/3 cup + grated cheddar cheese
1/3 cup chopped onion
2 large carrots, chopped
2 stalks celery, chopped
2 bay leaves
5 cups chopped dandelion leaves
2 tablespoons freshly squeezed lemon juice

1. Season the outside and inside of the chicken with salt and pepper. Place in a large pot.

2. Add carrots, celery, and bay leaves. Add enough water to completely cover the chicken. Place the pot over medium high heat and bring to a boil. Gently boil for 30 minutes.

3. Turn off the heat and cover. Allow to sit for 60 minutes.

4. Remove the chicken and take the meat off the bones. Cover with foil and set aside.

5. Put the bones back in the pot and cover partially. Bring to a gentle boil over medium high and gently boil for 2 hours.

6. Strain the resulting stock and throw away all the solids. Clean the pot and pour the stock back in it. Bring to a boil over medium high heat.

7. Add the dandelion leaves and boil for 15 minutes.

8. In the meantime, in a bowl, stir together the beef, egg, basil, zest, 1/3 cup Cheddar, onion, and salt and pepper to taste. Using your hands, turn this mixture into balls of about ½ inch around.

9. Add the meat balls and the juice to the soup. Cook for 4 minutes.

10. To serve, place some bite-sized pieces of chicken into serving bowls. Spoon the broth over the top. Add some meatballs. Sprinkle with cheese.

Serves 4 - 6.

Dandelions and Chickpeas

2 cups chickpeas (garbanzo beans), drained
4 cups dandelion leaves
3 tablespoons olive oil
4 cloves garlic, chopped fine
1/2 teaspoon red pepper flakes
juice and zest (grated peel) from 1 lime
Salt

1. Place a skillet over medium high heat and add the olive oil. Once warm, add the garlic and red pepper flakes. Sauté for 20 seconds. Reduce heat to medium

2. Add the dandelion leaves and stir until they are well coated with oil. Cover and cook for 2 minutes, or until the leaves are tender.

3. Pour the beans into a large bowl. Add the dandelion mixture. Add the lime juice and zest and season with a pinch or two of salt. Toss again.

Serves 2 – 4.

Balsamic Fried Eggs and Dandelion Greens

2 tablespoons olive oil
1 medium garlic clove, chopped fine
¾ cup dandelion leaves, chopped coarsely
4 eggs
1/4 cup balsamic vinegar

1. Pour 1 tablespoon of oil into a skillet placed over medium heat. Once warmed, add the garlic and sauté for 30 seconds.

2. Add the dandelion leaves; season with salt and pepper. Sauté for 1 minute, or until just wilted.

3. Immediately remove the skillet from the stove and spoon the leaves onto two serving plates.

4. Wipe out the skillet and add 1 tablespoon olive oil. Place over medium heat. Once the oil is warmed, add the eggs and fry for about 3 minutes, or until set and browned around the edges.

5. Add the vinegar and keep cooking until it becomes syrupy, about 2 minutes.

6. Place two eggs on each plate, on top of the greens. Spoon the vinegar reduction over each.

Serves 2.

Dandelion Salad with Pancetta

4 oz. pancetta, thinly sliced into ribbons (or 6 strips of bacon)
½ lb. dandelion leaves, chopped
1 garlic clove, minced
1 tablespoon freshly squeezed lemon juice
2 eggs, hardboiled
2 tablespoons olive oil
1 cup croutons
Salt
Pepper

1. Place a skillet over medium high heat. Once warmed, add the pancetta. Stir constantly and cook until crisp. Drain on paper towels.

2. Place the dandelion leaves in a salad bowl. Add the garlic and toss. Add the juice and toss. Drizzle with oil and toss. Add the croutons and pancetta and toss. Season with salt and pepper.

3. Slice the eggs and sprinkle over the top of the salad.

Serves 2 – 4.

Dandelion Pesto

Use this pesto just like you'd use traditional basil pesto – on top of pasta, as a pizza sauce, as a sandwich spread, as a seasoning for meat…

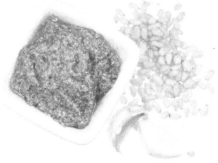

12 oz. dandelion leaves
1 cup olive oil
4 garlic cloves, peeled
6 tablespoons lightly toasted pine nuts
1 1/2 teaspoons salt
2 1/2 oz. Parmesan cheese, grated

1. Place 1/3 of the dandelion leaves in a food processor or blender. Add the olive oil. Chop for about 1 minute.

2. Scrape down the sides of the food processor and add another 1/3 of the leaves. Chop for about 1 minute. Repeat with the last 1/3 of the leaves until the leaves are chopped fine.

3. Add the garlic, pine nuts, salt, and Parmesan. Puree.

4. Season with salt, if needed. If the pesto seems to thick, add a little olive oil or water. Refrigerate for up to 4 days or freeze for up to 6 months.

Makes about 2 cups.

Dandy Soup

1 cup diced celery
1 cup diced carrot
1 cup diced onion
4 tablespoons minced fresh basil (or 4 teaspoons dried basil)
2 tablespoons minced fresh oregano (or 2 teaspoons dried oregano)
1 tablespoon cumin
4 garlic cloves, minced
1 tablespoon olive oil
4 cups chopped dandelion leaves
4 cups chopped spinach
8 cups chicken stock
1 bay leaf
1 cup fresh or frozen corn kernels
2 cups cooked Cannellini or Great Northern
1 cup diced potato
Salt
Pepper

1. Pour the oil into a large pot placed over medium high heat. Once warmed, add the onion, celery, carrot, garlic, basil, oregano, and cumin. Sauté until the vegetables are tender.

2. Add the stock, bay leaf, corn, beans, and potatoes. Simmer until potatoes are tender. Season with salt and pepper.

Serves 4.

Adapted from a recipe in Annie B. Bon's True Food: Eight Simple Steps for a Healthier You.

Creamy Dandelion Gratin

1/2 teaspoon butter
Salt
1 lb. dandelion leaves, cooked
1 cup coarse breadcrumbs
3 tablespoons + 1/4 cup freshly grated Parmesan cheese
1 1/3 cups heavy cream
2 garlic cloves, minced
1/4 teaspoon lemon zest (grated peel)
Pepper
1 1/2 oz. goat cheese (or ricotta)

1. Place a rack in the center of the oven and preheat to 375 degrees F. Butter a 5 cup gratin dish with butter; set aside.

2. Lay a clean kitchen towel on a rimmed baking sheet and spread the leaves on top. Roll up the kitchen towel (with the leaves inside) and press to remove excess moisture.

3. In a bowl, stir together the breadcrumbs, 3 tablespoons of Parmesan, and a pinch of salt.

4. In a saucepan placed over medium high heat, pour the cream and garlic. As soon as the mixture comes to a vigorous boil, remove the pan from the stove. Set aside for 10 minutes, then stir in the zest. Season with salt and pepper.

5. Chop up the dandelion leaves and place in a large bowl. Add 1/4 cup of Parmesan and the goat cheese. Mix well.

6. Spread the mixture in the prepared gratin dish. Pour the cream over the mixture, then stir. Season with additional salt and pepper. Sprinkle breadcrumbs over the top.

7. Bake about 30 minutes, or until there is a brown ring around the edge of the gratin.

Serves 4.

Adapted from a recipe in the May 6, 2010 issue of Fine Cooking.

Chipotle Dandelion Soup

4 cups chicken stock
4 cups water
Zest and juice from 1 lime
4 oz. fresh chorizo pork sausage, casings removed
1/2 cup fine cornmeal
1/2 cup finely chopped green onions (scallions)
1/2 cup chopped fresh cilantro
1 egg
2 garlic cloves, minced
1 teaspoon dried oregano
Pepper
1 1/4 lbs. ground beef
6 cups chopped dandelion leaves
1 cup sliced carrots
1 chipotle chile, minced
1 cup fresh or frozen corn kernels

1. Pour the stock and water into a Dutch oven placed over medium high heat. Bring to a simmer.

2. Place the sausage into a large mixing bowl and break it up with your hands. Stir in the cornmeal, green onions, cilantro, egg, garlic, oregano, lime zest, and some pepper. Stir in the beef. Scoop up 1 tablespoon of the mixture and form it into a meatball. Continue making meatballs until the mixture is used up.

3. To the stock mixture, add the dandelion leaves, carrots, and pepper. Gently add the meatballs. Simmer until the meatballs are thoroughly cooked through and the vegetables are tender, about 12 minutes. Add the corn and cook another 2 minutes. Stir in the lime juice.

Serves 4 – 6.

Adapted from a recipe in the March/April 2012 issue of Eating Well.

DIY Chorizo

1 lb. spicy pork sausage
2 tablespoons cider vinegar
2 teaspoons chopped fresh cilantro
2 teaspoons chili powder
1 garlic clove, minced
1/2 teaspoon ground cumin

1. In a large bowl, stir together the sausage (breaking up chunks), vinegar, cilantro, chili powder, garlic, and cumin. Freeze any leftovers.

Makes about 20 oz.

Dandelion Greens with Pine Nuts

Olive oil
1 garlic clove, finely chopped
1 lb. dandelion leaves, chopped
Salt
Pepper
3 tablespoons toasted pine nuts
3 tablespoon dried currants (optional)

1. Pour about a tablespoon of oil in a skillet placed over medium high heat. Once warmed, add the garlic and sauté about 30 seconds.

2. Add the dandelion leaves, one handful at a time, sautéing and wilting each handful before adding more. Season with salt and pepper. Sauté until the leaves are tender but slightly crisp.

3. Add the pine nuts and, if using, the currants, and cook another minute.

4. Transfer to a serving dish and drizzle with olive oil.

Serves 2 - 4.

Adapted from a recipe in the March 2010 issue of Sunset.

Dandelion Colcannon

2/3 - 3/4 cup hot mashed potatoes
1 tablespoon horseradish
1 tablespoon butter
1/2 cup shredded Co-Jack or Cheddar cheese
1 cup chopped dandelion leaves
1 - 2 tablespoons olive oil
1 garlic clove, minced
1 shallot, chopped
1/2 cup garbanzo beans, drained
Salt
Pepper

1. Place the mashed potatoes in a large serving bowl and stir in the horseradish, butter, cheese, salt and pepper. Season with salt and pepper.

2. Pour the oil into a small skillet placed over medium high heat. Once warmed, add the shallot and sauté for 1 minute.

3. Add the dandelion leaves and sauté until tender.

4. Add the garlic and garbanzo beans. Season with salt and pepper.

5. Stir the dandelion leaf mixture into the potato mixture, reheating if needed. Add a little butter, stirring in until melted.

Serves 2.

Adapted from a recipe at HeartSeaseCottage.typepad.com.

Chinese-Style Dandelion Dumplings

2 lbs. ground pork
2 cups minced dandelion leaves
3 cups minced Napa cabbage
1/2 cup minced bok choy leaves
5 green onions (scallions; divided), minced
1 tablespoon + 1 teaspoon minced fresh ginger
5 garlic cloves (divided), minced
8 oz. canned bamboo shoots, drained and minced
3 tablespoons + 1/2 cup low sodium soy sauce
Salt
Pepper
2 teaspoons (divided) granulated sugar
4 teaspoons sesame oil
1 egg white
1 tablespoon water
100 wonton wrappers
Coconut or olive oil
2 teaspoons chili oil

For the Dipping Sauce:
3 tablespoons hoisin sauce
4 teaspoons sesame oil
3 tablespoons balsamic vinegar

1. In a large bowl, combine the pork, dandelion leaves, cabbage, bok choy, 4 green onions, 1 tablespoon ginger, 3 cloves of garlic, bamboo shoots, 3 tablespoons soy sauce, a little salt and pepper, 1 teaspoon of sugar, and sesame oil. Chill overnight in the refrigerator.

2. In a small bowl, whisk together the egg white and water. Set aside.

3. Place 1 tablespoon of the pork mixture into a wonton wrapper, being sure to keep the remaining wrappers covered with a moist kitchen towel. With a pastry brush, brush the edges of the wrapper with the egg white mixture. Fold; seal the edges. Repeat with the remaining wrappers and pork mixture.

4. Place 2 tablespoons oil in a skillet placed over medium high heat. Once the oil melts, work in batches and place the wonton-wrapped dumplings in the skillet, seam side up. Cook until browned, about 30 to 60 seconds.

5. Pour 1/2 cup of water into the skillet; cover. Steam the dumplings about 7 minutes, or until the liquid in the skillet begins sizzling.

6. When the water evaporates, turn the dumplings over and keep cooking to brown the opposite side.

7. Make the dipping sauce: Combine chili oil, hoisin sauce, 1/2 cup of soy sauce, sesame oil, 1 teaspoon of sugar, balsamic vinegar, 1 teaspoon of ginger, 1 minced green onion, and 2 cloves of garlic.

Makes 100 dumplings.

Adapted from a recipe by AllRecipes.com's Challena.

Dandelion Spaghetti

Adding greens to a familiar dish like spaghetti is a great way to introduce dandelion leaves to less adventurous eaters. If serving this dish to children, I suggest chopping the leaves fine.

½ lb. spaghetti (uncooked)
1 bunch (about a large handful) dandelion leaves
3 strips bacon
1 shallot, sliced thin
2 garlic cloves, sliced thin
1/3 cup finely chopped bread
2 eggs, beaten
¼ teaspoon crushed red pepper flakes
1 cup shredded Parmesan

1. Fill a large pot with water and place over medium high heat. Bring to a boil and add the spaghetti. Cook until just tender, adding the dandelion leaves about 5 minutes before the pasta is done. Drain.

2. In a skillet placed over medium high heat, cook the bacon. Drain on a paper towel. Keep the drippings in the pan.

3. Add the shallot to the skillet and sauté until translucent. Using a slotted spoon, transfer the shallot to a large serving bowl.

4. Add the garlic to the skillet and sauté for 30 seconds. Add the bread. Stir once in a while until the bread is crispy and brown. Drain on paper towels.

5. To the serving bowl, add the beaten eggs, red pepper flakes, most of the shredded cheese, and half of the bacon, broken into bite-sized pieces. Add the pasta and toss. Season with salt and pepper, then add the rest of the bacon, the bread crumbs, and the remaining cheese. Toss to combine.

Serves 2.

Dandelion Salad with Tomato Dressing

For the Dressing:
1/4 cup crumbled goat cheese (or Feta)
2 tablespoons white wine vinegar
2 teaspoons pure maple syrup

1/4 cup olive oil
2 plum or cherry tomatoes, chopped
Salt
Pepper
1 tablespoon chopped fresh tarragon

For the Salad:
8 oz. uncooked pasta shells
2 slices bacon
1 tablespoon oil
1 medium red onion, sliced thin
2 cups chopped dandelion leaves
2 cups baby spinach (or torn regular spinach)
1/4 cup freshly grated Parmesan cheese

1. Make the dressing first: In a food processor or blender, combine the goat cheese, vinegar, and maple syrup. Add 1/4 cup oil and the tomatoes and blend until smooth. Season with salt and pepper. Fold in the tarragon. Set aside.

2. Fill a large saucepan with water and place over medium high heat. Bring to a boil and add the pasta. Cook until just tender; drain.

3. In a skillet placed over medium high heat, cook the bacon. Drain on paper towels. Keep the drippings in the skillet.

4. Add the onion to the skillet and sauté until translucent. Use a slotted spoon to transfer the onion to a large serving bowl. Crumble the bacon and add it to the bowl.

5. Once the onion-bacon mixture is cool, add the dandelion leaves, spinach, cheese, and ½ cup of the dressing. Toss. Serve the salad with extra dressing on the side.

Serves 2.

Adapted from a recipe in the October 27, 2011 edition of The Huffington Post.

Dandelion with Roasted Garlic Dressing

For the Dressing:
1 large head garlic, roasted
3 tablespoons olive oil
2 tablespoons balsamic vinegar
1 tablespoon freshly squeezed lime juice
Salt
Pepper

For the Salad:
1 medium shallot, chopped fine
6 cups chopped dandelion leaves
1/4 cup pine nuts, toasted
2 oz. goat (or Feta) cheese, crumbled
Pepper

1. Begin by making the dressing: Squeeze the roasted garlic pulp into a food processor or blender, throwing away the skins. Add the oil, vinegar, juice, and a little salt and pepper. Process until smooth.

2. Pour the dressing into a saucepan placed over medium heat and warm for about 2 minutes. Add the shallot. Simmer until softened.

3. Put the dandelion leaves in a large serving bowl. Pour the warm dressing over the leaves and toss until they are wilted. Add the pine nuts and goat cheese; toss. Season with pepper.

Serves 2 – 4.

Adapted from a recipe in the October 27, 2010 issue of The Huffington Post.

How To Roast Garlic

Rub your fingers over the head of garlic, removing the easy-to-remove paper-like skin. Do not separate the cloves. Place the head of garlic on a cutting board, on it's side, and cut off the tips of the cloves. Place the garlic head on a foil square and drizzle with about 1 tablespoon of olive oil. Wrap the foil around the garlic head and place in baking dish. Place in a preheated 400 degree F. oven until the garlic is tender, about 40 to 60 minutes. Unwrap and allow to cool some before adding to this recipe.

Dandelion Leaves and Bacon Dressing

7 slices bacon
2 eggs, beaten
1/2 cup granulated sugar
1/2 teaspoon salt
1 cup mayonnaise
1/3 cup apple cider vinegar
1 1/2 cups milk
3 tablespoons all purpose flour
3/4 pound chopped dandelion leaves

1. In a skillet placed over medium heat, fry the bacon. Drain on paper towels. Reserve 3 tablespoons of the drippings.

2. In a bowl, whisk together the eggs, sugar, salt, mayonnaise, vinegar, and milk.

3. To the bacon drippings in the skillet add the flour, whisking until smooth. Stirring constantly, cook until flour is browned, about 10 minutes.

4. Little by little, whisk in the liquid. Bring to a boil, whisking constantly. Crumble the bacon and add it to the skillet. Add the dandelion leaves. Cook and stir until the leaves are wilted.

Serves 2.

Dandelion Minestrone Soup

2 tablespoons+ olive oil
3 oz. chopped pancetta (or 5 - 6 slices bacon)
1 onion, diced
1 cup diced celery
4 garlic cloves, minced
4 cups chicken or beef stock
2+ cups water
28 oz. crushed tomatoes
1 cup pinto beans
2 cups chopped cabbage
15 oz. garbanzo beans, drained
½ teaspoon red pepper flakes
1 teaspoon Italian seasoning
1 bunch (about 1 large handful) dandelion leaves, chopped
2/3 cup uncooked macaroni pasta
Salt
Pepper
Freshly grated Parmesan cheese

1. In a large pot, heat 2 tablespoons olive oil over medium-high heat. Add the pancetta and cook until it starts browning.

2. Add the onions and celery, cooking until the onions begin turning translucent.

3. Add the minced garlic and cook for 1 minute.

4. Add the stock, water, and tomatoes, and bring to a simmer.

5. Add the beans, cabbage, red pepper flakes, Italian seasoning, and a little salt. Bring to a simmer and cook for about 35 minutes. Add more water if the soup becomes too thick.

6. Add the dandelion leaves to the bean mixture, simmering about 15 minutes, or until tender. Season with salt and pepper.

7. Add the pasta to the bean mixture and simmer until tender.

8. Serve soup with a sprinkling of Parmesan cheese and, if desired, parsley.

Serves 6.

Adapted from a recipe by AllRecipes.com's Chef John.

DIY Italian Seasoning

3 tablespoons dried basil
3 tablespoons dried oregano
3 tablespoons dried parsley
1 tablespoon garlic powder
1 teaspoon onion powder
1 teaspoon dried thyme
1 teaspoon dried rosemary
1/4 teaspoon black pepper
1/4 teaspoon red pepper flakes

Mix together and store in an air tight container in a cool, dark, dry location.

Dandy Potato Salad

5 lbs. white potatoes, peeled and cubed
3 tablespoons butter
Salt
Pepper
½ lb - 1 lb. bacon, diced
1 lb. chopped dandelion leaves
1 medium onion, diced
1 egg
1/2 cup white vinegar
1 tablespoon granulated sugar
1 tablespoon all purpose flour

1. Fill a large pot with water and place over medium high heat. Bring to a boil. Add the potatoes and cook until tender. Drain. Add the butter and toss until it's melted. Season with salt and pepper.

2. Cook the bacon in a skillet placed over medium heat. Drain on paper towels; set aside and reserve pan drippings.

3. In a large bowl, toss the dandelion leaves and onion together.

4. In another bowl, whisk together the egg, vinegar, and sugar. Season with salt and pepper.

5. Place the skillet with the bacon drippings back on medium high heat. Once warm, add the egg mixture. Crumble the bacon and add it to the skillet. Add the flour and whisk for 1 minute, or until thickened slightly.

6. Pour the bacon mixture over the dandelion leaf mixture and toss. On each plate, place some of the potatoes, then spoon the leaf mixture over them.

Serves 4 – 6.

Grilled Dandelions, Bacon, and Cheese Sandwiches

4 slices bacon
4 tablespoons butter
1 onion, sliced into thin strips
1/3 cup dry white wine or chicken stock
3 cups chopped dandelion leaves
2 teaspoons wine vinegar
Salt
Pepper
3 eggs
1 cup milk
3 tablespoons freshly grated Parmesan cheese
8 (1/2 inch thick) slices sourdough bread
4 teaspoons Dijon mustard (optional)
1/2 pound thinly sliced Gruyère or Swiss cheese

1. In a skillet placed over medium heat, cook the bacon. Drain on paper towels.

2. Place a large, heavy saucepan over medium high heat and add 2 tablespoons of butter. Once melted, add the onions. Sauté until soft and golden.

3. Add the white wine. Scrap the bottom of the pan and stir often. Once the wine is nearly absorbed, add the dandelion leaves and cook until wilted.

4. Remove the pan from the stove and add the vinegar, stirring to combine. Season with salt and pepper. Crumble the bacon and stir it in. Taste and add more vinegar, if desired.

5. In a medium mixing bowl, whisk together the eggs and milk. Stir in the Parmesan. Season with salt and pepper. Pour into a shallow dish.

6. Place the bread slices in the egg mixture, soaking each side. Very gently, brush the mustard over one side of the 4 pieces of bread. On the other pieces of bread, place a slice of Gruyère. On top of the cheese, place some onions, dandelion leaves, and crumbled bacon. Press a mustard-coated slice of bread on top.

7. Place 2 tablespoons of butter into a large skillet placed over medium high heat. Once melted, reduce the heat to low. Add one of the sandwiches, cover, and fry one side until golden and crispy. Carefully turn the sandwich and brown the opposite side.

Serves 4.

Adapted from a recipe in the January 27, 2011 issue of The Los Angeles Times.

Savory Dandelion Pie

Spring green pies are traditional in many parts of the world. If you've never had one, think of this dish as a less-rich quiche.

1½ lb. Swiss chard, chopped
½ lb. spinach, chopped
¾ lb. dandelion leaves, chopped
3 tablespoons butter
1 tablespoon olive oil
1 small onion, minced
2 garlic cloves, minced
½ small sweet pepper, chopped fine
2 small zucchini, grated
⅓ cup chopped fresh basil
¼ cup chopped fresh parsley
Salt
Pepper
3 eggs, beaten lightly
¼ cup freshly grated Parmesan cheese

¼ cup grated Swiss cheese
¼ cup breadcrumbs

1. Preheat the oven to 375 degrees F.

2. Place 1 tablespoon of butter in a medium saucepan placed over medium high heat. Once melted, add the garlic and sauté for 30 seconds. Add the onion and pepper and cook until just tender.

3. Stir in the chard, arugula, dandelion leaves, zucchini, basil, and parsley. Season with salt and pepper. Cover and cook, over medium, until tender, about 15 minutes.

4. Remove the cover and cook, stirring often, until the liquid is evaporated, about 25 minutes. Transfer to a large bowl.

5. Beat the eggs into the greens. Pour into the prepared pan. Sprinkle Parmesan and Swiss over the top.

6. In a small skillet placed over medium heat, melt 2 tablespoons butter. Stir in the breadcrumbs, sautéing until golden. Spread over the top of the pie and bake 25 minutes. Allow to stand for 10 minutes before cutting or serving.

4 - 6 servings.

Dandelion Gumbo

"Green gumbo" traditionally uses whatever greens happen to be available – including dandelion leaves.

1 cup peanut or coconut oil
1 cup all purpose flour
2 cups chopped onion
1 cup chopped bell pepper
1 cup chopped celery
4 garlic cloves
2 bay leaves
1 tablespoons Cajun seasoning (see below)
10 cups ham, pork, beef, or chicken stock
14 cups dandelion leaves or assorted dark, leafy greens

Salt
1 lb. andouille sausage (optional)

For the Cajun Seasoning:
1 teaspoon black pepper
1 teaspoon cayenne
1 teaspoon celery seed
1 teaspoon dried thyme
2 teaspoons dried oregano
1 tablespoon garlic powder
2 tablespoons paprika

1. In a pot placed over medium heat, warm the peanut or coconut oil for 2 minutes. Whisk in the flour until combined and lump free. Reduce the heat to medium low and cook, stirring constantly, until the sauce is browned

2. When the sauce is browned, add the onions, celery, and pepper. Reduce the heat to medium and cook, stirring once in a while, until the vegetables are tender.

3. Pour the stock into a different pot and bring to a simmer over medium high heat.

4. To the sauce, add the garlic; cook 1 minute. Add the bay leaves and the Cajun spice. A little at a time, add the stock. Cook and stir constantly until smooth. Add the dandelion leaves. Season with salt and pepper. Cover and gently simmer for 1 hour, 15 minutes.

4 Add the sausage, if using, and cook another 15 minutes.

Serves 10 - 12.

Dandelion and Vegetable Lasagna

1 large zucchini (or cooked lasagna noodles)
½ lb – 1 lb. dandelion leaves, cooked

For the Sauce:
3 tablespoons olive oil
1 medium bell pepper, chopped
1 medium onion, chopped
3 garlic cloves, minced
1/4 cup chopped fresh parsley
28 oz. cut up tomatoes
12 oz. tomato paste
2 bay leaves
1 teaspoon dried basil leaves
1 teaspoon dried oregano leaves

For the Cheese Mixture:
1/4 cup freshly grated Parmesan cheese
15 oz. ricotta cheese
2 large eggs
1/4 teaspoon pepper

For the Topping:
12 oz. mozzarella cheese, shredded
1/4 cup freshly grated Parmesan cheese

1. Preheat oven to 350 degrees F.

2. Pour the oil into a large skillet and place over medium high heat. Once warmed, add the green pepper, onion, and garlic. Sauté until vegetables are tender.

3. Add the parsley, tomatoes (undrained), tomato paste, bay leaves, basil, and oregano. Keep cooking, stirring occasionally, until the sauce comes to a full boil. Reduce the heat and cook, stirring occasionally, 30 minutes on low heat. Remove the bay leaves.

4. While the sauce is reducing, mix 1/4 cup Parmesan cheese, ricotta cheese, eggs, and pepper in a medium bowl. Refrigerate.

5. If using, slice zucchini into thin (about 1/4 inch) strips, down the length of the vegetable.

6. When the sauce finishes reducing, spread 1 cup of the sauce on the bottom of a 13 x 9 inch baking dish. Lay zucchini slices all across the top of the sauce, just like you'd do with traditional lasagna noodles. (Or use cooked lasagna noodles.) Over this, place a layer of dandelion leaves. Spread 1/3 of the cheese mixture over this. Repeat layers. End with cheese.

7. Bake for about 30 minutes, or until heated through and bubbly. Allow to stand for about 10 minutes.

6 – 8 servings.

Pork, White Bean and Dandelion Soup

1 tablespoon olive oil
1 lb. pork tenderloin, cut into 1 inch pieces
Salt
Pepper
1 medium onion, minced
4 garlic cloves, minced
2 teaspoons paprika
1/4 teaspoon crushed red pepper
1 cup white wine or chicken stock

4 plum or cherry tomatoes, chopped
4 cups chicken stock
8 cups chopped dandelion leaves
15 oz. white beans, drained

1. Place a Dutch oven over medium high heat. Add the oil. Once warmed, add the pork. Season with salt and pepper. Cook, stirring once in a while, until the pork is no longer pink on the outside. Use a slotted spoon to transfer the pork to a plate.

2. Add the onion to the Dutch oven. Cook, stirring frequently, until golden.

3. Add the garlic, paprika, and red pepper. Stir and cook for 30 seconds. Add the wine and tomatoes. Increase the heat to high. Scrape the bottom of the pot and stir. Add stock and bring to a boil.

4. Stir in the dandelion leaves and cook until wilted.

5. Reduce the heat and simmer, stirring now and then, until the leaves are tender, about another 4 minutes.

7. Stir in the beans, the pork (and any juices on the plate that held them). Simmer until everything is heated through, about another 3 to 5 minutes.

Serves 4 - 6.

Dandelion and Potato Hash

2 tablespoons horseradish
1 medium shallot, minced
Salt
Pepper
8 cups chopped dandelion leaves, cooked
2 cups hash browns
3 tablespoons olive oil

1. In a large bowl, stir together the horseradish, shallot, and a little salt and pepper. Stir in the dandelion leaves (cooled) and hash browns.

3. Pour the oil in a skillet placed over medium heat. Once warmed, add the leaf mixture, spread evenly on the bottom of the skillet. Cook, stirring every 2 or 3 minutes then spreading the mixture out evenly again, until the hash browns turn crisp and golden.

Serves 2 – 4.

Dandy Omelet

Olive oil
1 small onion, diced
4 garlic cloves, minced
2 cups chopped dandelion leaves
1 teaspoon paprika
Salt
2 eggs
¼ cup grated cheddar or mozzarella cheese

1. Place a skillet over medium high heat and add about a tablespoon of olive oil. Once warmed, add the onion and garlic and sauté until the onion is translucent.

2. Add the dandelion leaves and sauté until wilted. With a slotted spoon, transfer the dandelion mixture to a bowl and set aside.

3. Crack the eggs into the skillet and scramble with a fork. Cook until the eggs are firm, then sprinkle the cheese and leaf mixture over the top. Flip one half of the omelet over the greens.

Serves 1.

Variation: Begin by frying some bacon strips in the skillet; drain on paper towels. Sauté the onion, garlic, and leaves in the bacon dripping. When adding the filling to the omelet, crumble the bacon in, too. Other good additions include sliced mushrooms, diced tomato, cooked hash browns, or other types of cheese.

Dandelion Leaf Swirl Bread

1 lb. dandelion leaves, cooked and chopped
2 garlic cloves, minced
¼ cup + olive oil
Pepper
Freshly grated Parmesan or mozzarella cheese
3 – 4 lbs. all purpose flour (about 10 – 13 cups)
5 teaspoons salt
2 oz. cake yeast (or 10 teaspoons or 1 oz. of dry active yeast)

1. Pour the dandelion leaves in a bowl and stir in the garlic, oil, and some pepper. Stir in a handful of cheese. Set aside.

2. In a separate bowl. combine 4 cups lukewarm water, 3 lbs. (about 10 cups) flour, salt, and yeast. If the dough seems too wet, add a little more flour.

3. Onto a lightly floured counter or other smooth work surface, roll out the dough so it's about ¼ inch thick. Spoon the dandelion leaf mixture evenly over the top. Roll the dough into a log. Brush the top with garlic, cover, and allow to rise in a warm location for 20 minutes.

4. In the meantime, preheat the oven to 350 degrees F. When the bread is done rising, bake it until golden, about 15 – 20 minutes.

Makes 1 loaf.

Adapted from a recipe in Peter A. Gail's Dandelion Celebration.

Dandelion Spoon Bread

12 oz. pearl onions
1 cup heavy cream
2 bay leaves
1 tablespoon chopped fresh parsley
1 garlic clove, minced
1/2 teaspoon freshly grated nutmeg
Salt
Pepper
1 cup chicken stock
2 cups dandelion leaves, cooked and drained
1 cup sour cream
2 eggs
Salt
8.5 oz. corn bread mix
½ cup melted butter
Shredded Swiss cheese

1. Preheat the oven to 350 degrees F. Grease a 1 ½ quart casserole dish; set aside. Fill a clean sink or large bowl with ice water.

2. Fill a large pot with water and place over medium high heat. Bring to a boil and add the pearl onions, cooking for 1 minute. Drain and place in ice water. Once cooled, discard the onion skins.

3. In a saucepan placed over medium heat, place the onions, cream, bay leaves, parsley, garlic, and nutmeg. Simmer, covered, for 10 minutes, stirring once in a while, until thickened.

4. Add the stock and season with salt and pepper. Keep cooking for another 5 minutes, then remove from the stove. Remove the bay leaves. Set aside.

5. In a large mixing bowl, combine the onion mixture, dandelion leaves, eggs, sour cream, butter, and a little salt.

6. Add the cornbread mix, stirring well to combine. Pour into the prepared casserole dish and bake until a toothpick inserted in the center comes out clean, about 30-35 minutes.

7. Sprinkle the Swiss cheese over the top of the casserole and bake another 2 minutes, or until the cheese is melted. Serve warm.

Serves 6 - 8.

Adapted from a recipe in Peter A. Gail's Dandelion Celebration.

DIY Cornbread Mix

**Make the above recipe even more healthy by using your own homemade corn bread muffin mix:
http://goo.gl/5jhmi**

Dandy Bread Spread
The Italians often serve dandelion leaves with bread. This recipe is ideal as an appetizer.

½ lb. dandelion leaves
10 oz. cream cheese, room temperature
2 oz. anchovy paste (or 3 anchovy fillets, minced)
Pepper
Crusty bread

1. In a food processor or blender, pulse the leaves, cream cheese, anchovies, and a bit of butter until smooth. Serve spread over bread.

Makes about 1 ½ cups.

Italian Dandelion Bread Topping

9 garlic cloves
¼ cup + 2 tablespoons olive oil
16 slices crusty bread
6 cups chopped dandelion leaves
Salt
Pepper
½ cup chopped Gruyere or Swiss cheese

1. In a small bowl, combine the olive oil with 3 minced garlic cloves. Set aside.

2. Toast the bread. (If the slices are too thick for your toaster, toast them in the oven's broiler, being sure to turn them over once.)

3. Once the toast is cool enough to handle (but still warm), brush one side of each piece of toast with a little of the olive oil mixture. Set aside.

4. Pour 2 tablespoons of oil in a skillet placed over low heat and add 4 mashed garlic cloves. Sauté for 1 minute. Add the dandelion leaves. Season with salt and pepper and turn up the heat to medium high. Sauté until the leaves are tender.

4. Transfer the greens to a serving bowl and pour any liquid into the skillet. Allow the dandelion leaves to cool slightly.

5. Sprinkle the leaves with cheese; toss to combine.

6. To serve, spoon the leaf mixture over the toast.

Serves 8 - 16.

Dandelion Enchiladas

28 oz. enchilada sauce
1 ½ cups dandelion leaves, cooked
3 greens onions (scallions), chopped
1/3 cup sour cream
1 1/2 cups shredded Co-Jack cheese
½ lb. cooked ground beef or cooked, shredded chicken breast
About 8 (7 inch) tortillas
Sliced black olives (optional)

1. Preheat the oven to 350 degrees F.

2. In a bowl, combine ½ cup enchilada sauce, dandelion leaves, onions, sour cream, and 1 cup cheese.

3. Spoon about ½ cup of enchilada sauce onto the bottom of an 11 x 7 inch baking dish.

4. Spoon about ¼ cup of the dandelion leaf mixture into a tortilla and roll up. Place, seam side down, in the baking dish. Repeat with remaining tortillas.

5. Spoon the remaining enchilada sauce over the rolled tortillas. Sprinkle remaining cheese over the top. If using, scatter sliced black olives over the top.

6. Bake until cheese is melted and filling is bubbly, about 20 minutes.

Serves 6 – 8.

Dandelion and Bacon Bread Pudding

Butter
3 1/2 cups whole milk
1 garlic clove, minced
Pepper
6 oz. bacon, chopped
1 tablespoon olive oil
9 cups chopped dandelion leaves
2 shallots, minced
6 eggs
8 oz. goat cheese (or ricotta)
8 cups stale bread, chopped into 1/2 inch pieces
1 tablespoon lemon zest (grated peel)

1. Preheat the oven to 375 degrees. Butter a 9 x 13 inch baking dish; set aside.

2. In a medium saucepan placed over high heat, stir together the milk, garlic, and pepper. Just before the milk comes to a simmer, remove the pan from the stove.

3. In a skillet placed over medium high heat, cook the bacon until nearly done. Add the olive oil, dandelion leaves, and shallot. Stir until the leaves are wilted. Remove the skillet from the stove.

4. Whisk the eggs in a large bowl. Add the now-cooled milk and the goat cheese; whisk to combine.

5. Add the bread, dandelion leaf mixture, and lemon zest; stir to combine. Pour the mixture into the prepared baking dish, pressing the bread down toward the bottom of the dish. Allow to sit for 15 minutes.

6. Bake until golden, about 35 minutes.

Serves 6 – 8.

Adapted from the October 17, 207 issue of The Los Angeles Times.

Balsamic Dandelions and Potatoes

6 slices bacon, chopped
4 green onions (scallions), diced
3 cups chopped dandelion leaves
¼ cup balsamic vinegar
2 tablespoons olive oil
Salt
½ teaspoon lemon pepper
4 cups warm mashed potatoes

1. In a skillet placed over medium high heat, cook the bacon. Drain on paper towels.

2. In a large serving bowl, toss together the bacon, onion, dandelion leaves, vinegar, oil, a pinch or two of salt, and the lemon pepper.

3. Toss in the mashed potatoes.

Serves 4 - 6.

Dandelion Fajitas
You can easily add dandelion leaves to almost any fajita recipe; here is one of my favorites.

15 oz. black beans (drained, if canned)
1 tablespoon olive oil
1/2 onion, chopped
2 garlic cloves, minced
4 mushrooms, sliced thin
1/2 sweet bell pepper, chopped
1 handful dandelion greens, chopped
1 tablespoon paprika
1 tablespoon chili powder

Salt
Pepper
Flour tortillas
Sour cream (optional)

1. Place a skillet over medium low heat and add the black beans. Sauté until warmed. Remove from the stove, cover, and keep warm.

2. Place a smaller skillet over medium low heat and add the olive oil. Once warmed, add the onions, garlic, bell pepper, and mushrooms. Sauté until the onion and pepper are tender.

3. Add the dandelion leaves, paprika, chili powder, and a little salt and pepper. Sauté until the leaves are wilted and tender.

4. In a bowl, combine the onion mixture with the black beans.

5. Spoon the mixture into flour tortillas and serve with sour cream on the side, if desired.

Serves 4.

Dandelion and Ham Hock Soup

Here's another very traditional way to cook dandelion leaves, with the ham hock adding just the right amount of additional flavor to the soup.

12 cups chopped dandelion leaves, cooked
1 ham hock
1 onion, sliced thin
2 garlic cloves, chopped
¼ teaspoon crushed red pepper
16 oz. cannellini or great northern beans, drained

1. In a Dutch oven placed over medium high heat, place the ham hock, onion, garlic, and red pepper. Add enough water to cover. Bring to a boil and boil gently until onion is tender.

2. Add the dandelion leaves and the beans. Return to a boil. Reduce the heat and simmer for 5 minutes.

3. Remove the ham hock and chop the meat. Place the meat back in the Dutch oven.

Serves 6 – 8.

Adapted from a recipe in Peter A. Gail's Dandelion Celebration.

Skillet Potatoes with Dandelions

Dandelion recipes go back as far as recipes have been written down. This "scramble" or "hash" has deep roots in American history. Our ancestors would have used whatever greens and vegetables were available.

2 – 4 strips bacon
1 1/2 lbs. potatoes, cut into 1 inch chunks
Salt
Pepper
1 cup dandelion leaves, chopped
1 garlic clove, sliced thin
Shredded cheese
Sour cream (optional)

1. Cook the bacon in a skillet placed over medium heat. Drain on paper towels. Reserve pan drippings.

2. Pour water into a medium saucepan. Add a pinch or two of salt. Place on medium high heat and bring to a boil. Add the potatoes. Reduce heat and simmer until the potatoes are tender.

3. Add the dandelion leaves and cook until wilted. Drain.

4. Place the skillet back on the stove over medium high heat. Once the pan drippings are warmed, add the potatoes and dandelion leaves. Cook, stirring often, until the potatoes are golden. Add the garlic; cook another minute. Season with salt and pepper.

5. To serve, sprinkle with cheese and, if desired, a dollop of sour cream.

Serves 2 - 4.

Dandelion Matzo Ball Soup

2 eggs
2 tablespoon oil
1 ½ cups matzo meal
Salt
12 cups + 2 tablespoon chicken stock
¼ cup diced carrots
¼ cup chopped onion
1 cup + ¼ chopped dandelion leaves
Croutons (optional)

1. In a bowl, whisk the eggs. Whisk in the oil.

2. Stir in the matzo meal, a pinch or two of salt, 2 tablespoons of stock, and ¼ cup dandelion leaves. Cover and refrigerate for 20 minutes.

3. Place a pot over medium high heat and add 12 cups of stock. Add the carrots, onion, and 1 cup of dandelion leaves. Bring to a boil.

4. Scoop up the chilled matzo mixture into a tablespoon and drop into the soup. Reduce the heat and boil gently for 30 to 40 minutes.

5. Serve topped with croutons, if desired.

Serves 6 – 8.

Adapted from a recipe in Peter A. Gail's Dandelion Celebration.

Dandelion and New Potato Gratin

Butter
2 garlic cloves, minced
1 1/2 lbs. new potatoes
2 cups coarsely chopped dandelion greens
Salt
Pepper
1 cup crème fraîche
1/3 cup whole milk
1 1/2 cups grated Gruyère (or Swiss) cheese

1. Preheat the oven to 375 degrees F. Butter a large gratin dish. Sprinkle the garlic over the bottom of the dish.

2. Slice the potatoes about ¼ inch thick. Overlap about ½ the potatoes on the bottom of the dish. Place the dandelion leaves over the potatoes and season with salt and pepper. Layer the remaining potato slices on top and season again with salt and pepper.

3. In a small mixing bowl, whisk together the crème fraîche and the milk. Pour over the potatoes. Sprinkle with cheese.

4. Bake until the potatoes are easy to pierce with a knife and the cheese is golden, about 45 minutes.

Serves 6 – 8.

Adapted from the April 2, 2008 issue of The Los Angeles Times.

Dandelion Tortellini Soup

3 – 5 cups cooked, diced chicken
½ lb. cooked ham, diced
2 sticks pepperoni, diced
1 onion, chopped
2 celery stalks, chopped
2 carrots, chopped
2 garlic cloves, chopped fine
5 lbs. dandelion leaves, cooked
½ lb. cheese-filled tortellini
1/2 cup + freshly grated Parmesan or Romano cheese

1. Place a pot over medium high heat and add 32 cups water, chicken, ham, pepperoni, onion, celery, carrots, and garlic. Bring to a boil and boil 2 minutes.

2. Add the dandelion leaves and return to a gentle boil.

3. Add the tortellini and cook until just tender.

4. Remove the soup from the stove and stir in the grated cheese. Serve with additional grated cheese on the side.

Serves 2 – 4.

Adapted from a recipe in Peter A. Gail's Dandelion Celebration.

Dandelion and Chicken Stir Fry

2 boneless, skinless chicken breasts, cut into 1/2 inch strips
1 teaspoon minced fresh, peeled ginger
1 garlic clove, minced
2 tablespoons low sodium soy sauce
1 tablespoon Worcestershire sauce
1 tablespoon olive oil
Pepper
About ½ lb. dandelion leaves
1 onion, minced

1. In a mixing bowl, stir together the chicken, ginger, garlic, soy sauce, and Worcestershire sauce until everything is well coated. Cover and refrigerate for 60 minutes.

2. Pour a tablespoon of oil into a skillet or wok and place over medium high heat.

3. Remove the chicken from the marinade, using a slotted spoon. Add to the skillet and cook until just beginning to turn golden. Add the onion. Cook and stir for 1 minute. Add the dandelion leaves and cook until the leaves are wilted. Season with pepper.

4. Pour the marinade into the skillet and stir to combine. Taste, adding additional soy or Worcestershire sauce, if desired.

Serves 2.

Dandelion-Stuffed Chicken

6 cups dandelion leaves

1/2 cup sour cream
1/2 cup shredded Pepper Jack cheese
4 cloves garlic, minced
4 skinless, boneless chicken breast halves, pounded to 1/2 inch thickness
Pepper
8 slices bacon

1. Preheat the oven to 375 degrees F.

2. Pour the dandelion leaves into a large bowl. Add the sour cream, cheese, and garlic; stir well.

3. Lay one chicken breast on a cutting board and spoon about 2 or 3 tablespoons of the leaf mixture into the center. Roll the chicken up (with the leaves on the inside) and "pin" closed with a toothpick.

4. Wrap two slices of bacon around the chicken. Place in a baking dish. Repeat with the remaining chicken.

5. Bake for 35 minutes, then increase the heat to 500 degrees F for 5 to 10 minutes, or until the bacon is browned.

Serves 4.

Dandelion Green Energy Drink

You can drink your dandelion leaves, too. This is a very simple, very healthy recipe.

6 dandelion leaves, chopped
4 cups water

1. Pour the water into a saucepan placed over medium high heat. Bring to a boil.

2. Add the dandelion leaves. Immediately remove from the heat and allow to cool in the pan. Once cooled, place in the refrigerator overnight.

3. The next day, remove the leaves. (You may add them to a salad or other dish, if desired.) Drink cold.

Dandelion and Fruit Smoothie

The sweetness of the fruits in this smoothie do a great job of making this drink appeal to almost anyone.

1 medium pear, cored
1 medium apple, cored
1 banana, peeled
1/2 cup fresh or frozen cranberries
4 cups of dandelion leaves

1. Place 8 oz. of water into a blender, then add the pear, apple, banana, and cranberries and pulse. Add the dandelion leaves and puree fully.

Adapted from a recipe at ChefRyanaBitz.wordpress.com.

Dandy Berry Smoothie

½ cup hulled strawberries
½ cup fresh or frozen blueberries
½ cup dandelion leaves
½ cup crushed ice
¼ cup plain yogurt
¼ cup milk
1 teaspoon coconut oil

1. Place all the ingredients in blender and puree until smooth.

Adapted from a recipe at FitSugar.com.

Dandelion Mix Smoothie

3 cups dandelion greens
2 cups spinach greens
1 banana
1 mango, peeled and seeded
1 apple, cored and quartered
1 cup strawberries, hulled
Juice from 1 lemon
2 cups water
1 cup ice

1. In a blender, pour all the ingredients and pulse until smooth.

Adapted from a recipe at Recipes.SparkPeople.com.

Dandelion Flowers:
Good for the Body – and Brain!

The sunny yellow flowers of the dandelion are completely edible and have some nice nutritional benefits. They contain vitamins A, C, and B, beta-carotene, zinc, potassium, and iron. Perhaps best of all, the flowers are a superb source of lecithin - which is believed to maintain brain function and may slow or stop Alzheimer's disease. Lecithin is also good for the liver.

Flavor

Dandelion petals by themselves have a very slight, sweet flavor. Some compare it to mild honey. In cooking, the petals tend to take on the flavors of the other ingredients in the dish. The green parts that hold the petals in place (the sepals) are bitter; many recipes call for removing them, but this is largely a matter of personal preference.

When to Harvest Dandelion Flowers

Dandelion flowers may be harvested any time the plant is blooming. For best results, snip off flower heads when they are freshest, in the morning. Avoid flowers that aren't fully opened, are beginning to turn brown or wilted, or are starting to lose their petals.

Preserving Dandelion Flowers

Dandelion flowers may be preserved through freezing or dehydrating.

Freezing: After harvesting the flower heads, allow them to sit outside for a few hours. Any insects in the flowers will crawl off. You may then either lay the flower heads on a rimmed baking sheet and place them in the freezer; when they are stiff, transfer them to a freezer bag. Or, remove the petals and place those in bags by themselves. Freeze for 6 months to a year and use only in cooked dishes or for making tea, jelly, or marmalade.

Dehydrating: For successful dehydrating, select flowers that have just opened. If you try to dehydrate older flowers, they will turn into white puff balls that spread the dandelion's seeds. Dehydrate the entire flower head in a dehydrator set at 95 to 105 degrees, until completely dry and crispy. Alternatively, place the flower heads on a wire cooling rack set inside a rimmed baking sheet; place in the oven, set at its lowest temperature, until completely dry. Allow to cool completely, then store in an air tight container in a cool, dark, dry location. Dehydrated flowers are most suitable for tea.

How to Remove Dandelion Flower Petals

Many recipes call for removing the petals from the bitter green parts (sepals) of the flower. In my experience, the quickest way to remove the petals is to hold the base of the flower in one hand and pinch the base of the flower head with the fingers on that hand. A gentle pull from the opposite hand will remove most of the yellow petals. You may also try rolling the base of the flower between your forefinger and thumb, which encourages the petals to fall off.

Another method is to hold the flower head in one hand and use scissors to snip off the petals at the base of the flower. Still another method is to hold the base of the flower with a strawberry huller and the petals of the flower with the opposite hand. Pinch and twist to remove the petals.

Whichever method you choose, removing the petals is a bit time consuming. With a single person working, it can take about an hour to get 4 cups of petals (enough to make dandelion jelly, for example). So find a comfy seat and something great to listen to. I usually make this project a family event; kids are great helpers when you're making fun food!

Also, do remember: Not all dandelion flower recipes call for removing the petals. In addition, you don't need to be type-A about petal removal; a few green sepals in the mix won't hurt anything.

Dandelion Jelly (Dandelion Honey)

Here's a superb introduction to eating dandelions. The resulting jelly tastes very much like honey.

4 cups dandelion petals
2 tablespoons freshly squeezed lemon juice
4 cups granulated sugar
1/2 teaspoon pure vanilla extract
6 tablespoons powdered pectin

1. Review the guidelines for using a boiling water bath canner. (You can find them at my blog: http://goo.gl/DNpto)

2. Dump the dandelion petals in a stainless steel pot. Add 8 cups of water and turn the heat to medium high. Bring to a boil and boil for 10 minutes.

3. Place a bowl on the counter or in the sink and set a fine strainer over it. Carefully pour the dandelion petal mixture through the strainer. Press down on the petals with the back of a spoon in order to extract as much of the golden liquid as possible. Discard the petals. (Don't put them down a garbage disposal because they form a tight clump that might clog it). Thoroughly clean the strainer, removing any petals that stick to it.

4. Place another bowl on the counter or in the sink. Place the strainer over it. Place a coffee filter inside the strainer. (If the strainer is large, use multiple coffee filters, to cover the whole surface of the strainer.) Carefully pour the strained dandelion liquid through the strainer again.

5. Clean the pot so there are no petals or debris in it. With a clean measuring cup, measure out 3 cups of the dandelion liquid and place it in the pot. Add the lemon juice, vanilla extract, and pectin. Bring to a full rolling boil that can't be stirred down with a spoon. Add the sugar and stir until dissolved.

6. Bring the mixture to a full boil and, stirring constantly, boil hard for 1 minute. Remove the pot from the stove.

7. Ladle the jelly into 8 oz. jelly jars, leaving 1/4 inch headspace. Wipe the rims of the jars with a damp, clean towel. Place lids and screwbands on the jars.

8. If desired, measure out another 3 cups of dandelion petal liquid and repeat steps 5 through 8. (If you try to double the recipe and use all the dandelion liquid at once, the jelly may be too runny.) Process jars for 10 minutes* in a boiling bath canner.

Every 3 cups of petal liquid fills about 4- 5 jelly jars.

Note: Any remaining dandelion petal liquid can be refrigerated for use in teas. Or, pour into ice cube trays and freeze for a sweet addition to iced tea.

* If you live at a high altitude, read this important information about adjusting canning times: http://goo.gl/ACFRb

No Sugar Added Dandelion Jelly

1 cup dandelion petals
12 oz. frozen 100 % white grape juice concentrate
2 oz. low sugar pectin

1. Review the guidelines for using a boiling water bath canner. (You can find them at my blog: http://goo.gl/DNpto)

2. Dump the dandelion petals in a stainless steel pot. Add 2 cups of water and turn the heat to medium high. Bring to a boil and boil for 10 minutes.

3. Place a bowl on the counter or in the sink and set a fine strainer over it. Carefully pour the dandelion petal mixture through the strainer. Press down on the petals with the back of a spoon in order to extract as much of the golden liquid as possible. Discard the petals. (Don't put them down a garbage disposal because they form a tight clump that might clog it). Thoroughly clean the strainer, removing any petals that stick to it.

 4. Place another bowl on the counter or in the sink. Place the strainer over it. Place a coffee filter inside the strainer. (If the strainer is large, use multiple coffee filters, to cover the whole surface of the strainer.) Carefully pour the strained dandelion liquid through the strainer again.

5. Clean the pot so there are no petals or debris in it. With a clean measuring cup, measure out 2 ½ cups of the dandelion liquid and place it in the pot. Add the juice and pectin. Bring to a full rolling boil that can't be stirred down with a spoon. Boil hard for 1 minute. Remove the pot from the stove.

7. Ladle the jelly into 8 oz. jelly jars, leaving 1/4 inch headspace. Wipe the rims of the jars with a damp, clean towel. Place the lids and screwbands on the jars.

8. Process jars for 10 minutes* in a boiling bath canner.

Fills about 4 jelly jars.

* If you live at a high altitude, read this important information about adjusting canning times: http://goo.gl/ACFRb

Dandelion Flower Marmalade

½ cup dandelion petals
2 cups. lemon and orange peel
2 cups apples, chopped into small pieces
3 cups granulated sugar

1. Review the guidelines for using a boiling water bath canner. (You can find them at my blog: http://goo.gl/DNpto)

2. In a large saucepan placed over medium heat, add the petals, peels, and apples. Add enough water to cover the mixture. Bring to a simmer and cook for 60 minutes.

3. Pour the mixture into a sieve lined with coffee filters and allow the liquid to drain into a bowl. Do not press. Allow to drip overnight.

4. Measure out 2 ½ cups of the strained liquid. Pour into a pot placed over medium high heat. Add the sugar and stir constantly, bringing to a boil that can't be stirred down.

5. Remove the pot from the stove and keep stirring until any foam on top has disappeared. Ladle into the prepared 8 oz. canning jars, leaving ¼ inch headspace; add lids and screwbands.

6. Process in a boiling water canner for 10 minutes*.

Note: Any remaining dandelion petal liquid can be refrigerated for use in teas. Or, pour into ice cube trays and freeze for a sweet addition to iced tea.

Fills about 4 – 5 jelly jars.

* If you live at a high altitude, read this important information about adjusting canning times: http://goo.gl/ACFRb

Dandelion Vinegar

Use this vinegar just like you would any vinegar. It's a great addition to salad dressings, in particular.

1 quart of dandelion flower heads
apple cider or white wine vinegar

1. Pack a glass quart-sized jar with the flower heads. Pour in enough vinegar to cover the flowers. Screw on a plastic lid* and keep in a cool, dark location for 4 weeks.

2. Line a sieve with paper coffee filters or a double layer of cheesecloth. Strain, throwing away the solids.

3. Pour the liquid into a clean glass jar and cap with a plastic lid.*

* Metal lids react negatively with vinegar, so it's important to use a plastic one.

Dandelion Flower Oil

This oil can be used in any recipe calling for olive oil.

1 cup dandelion petals
¾ cup olive oil

1. Pour oil into a saucepan placed over low heat. Add the petals. Simmer for 25 - 30 minutes. Remove from stove and allow to cool completely.

2. Strain through a sieve lined in coffee filters or two layers of cheesecloth. Pour into a glass jar with a well-fitting lid. Use within 3 weeks.

Dandelion Flower Omelet

This is a very mild and pleasing recipe. You probably won't taste the flower petals – but you'll still be taking advantage of their nutrition.

1 tablespoon olive oil
1 cup diced onion
1 cup button mushrooms, sliced
1 cup diced sweet pepper
2 cups dandelion petals
4 eggs, beaten
1 tablespoon olive oil
Salt
Pepper

1. Place a skillet over medium high heat and add the oil. Once warm, add the onions, mushrooms, and sweet pepper, cooking until the vegetables are tender. Transfer to a bowl, using a slotted spoon. Stir in the dandelion petals and allow the mixture to cool a few minutes.

2. In a separate bowl, beat the eggs. Add to the mushroom mixture.

3. Pour the mixture into the skillet. Season with salt and pepper. Once the egg is firm, fold the omelet in half and serve.

Serves 1.

Dandelion Flower Pickles

1 cup dandelion flowers
½ teaspoon sea salt
½ teaspoon granulated sugar
White wine vinegar

1. Place the flowers in a glass bowl; toss with the salt and sugar until well coated.

2. Pour the buds into a glass jar with a plastic lid.* Pour the vinegar over the buds. Secure the lid. Refrigerate for 2 weeks before eating.

* Metal lids react negatively with vinegar and therefore should not be used.

More Pickled Flowers...

Any of the pickled dandelion bud recipes (in the chapter on buds) work for opened flowers, too.

Just be sure to select the freshest, more-recently-opened flowers you can find.

Dandelion Flower Tea

This is a refreshing tea that may be served hot or cold.

About 8 dandelion flower heads*

1. Pour some water into a small saucepan and place over high heat.

2. Pack the flower heads into a tea ball. Close the ball and place it in a cup.

3. Once the water boils, pour it over the tea ball, into the cup. Steep for 10 – 15 minutes.

Variation: This tea may also be made with dehydrated flower heads.

* Most recipes for dandelion flower tea tell you to remove all the green parts of the flower head and discard them. But the resulting tea is nearly flavorless. Having the whole flower head steep in the tea water makes for a pleasing, mild, and slightly earthy flavor – plus it's more nutritious.

Dandelion Flower Iced Tea

Dandelion flower heads
Water
Tea bags of your choice (optional)

1. Fill a quart jar about 1/3 of the way with dandelion flower heads.

2. Pour some water in a saucepan and bring to a boil. Allow to cool a minute or two, then pour over the flowers, filling the jar. If desired, add tea bags of your choice.

3. Steep for at least 10 – 25 minutes, strain, and serve over ice.

Dandelion and Lime Iced Tea

1 cup hot water
½ cup dried red raspberry leaf (optional)
Freshly squeezed juice from 4 limes
4 cups dandelion petals
12 cups cold water
Honey or granulated sugar (optional)

1. Place the red raspberry leaf (if using) in a bowl and cover with the hot water. Allow to steep for 8 minutes. Strain.

2. Pour the resulting tea (or 1 cup of hot water) into a 1 gallon pitcher. Stir in the lime juice. Stir in the petals.

3. Refrigerate for at least 3 hours. Strain and sweeten with honey or sugar to taste, if desired.

Dandelion Flower Cookies

The first time I gave my children dandelions as food, I made these cookies. Sneaky, aren't I? But they loved them just as much as any cookie and the experience made them much more open to trying other dandelion dishes. (Want more tips for teaching children about wild food? Visit my blog: http://goo.gl/uW39a)

1/2 cup butter, at room temperature
3/4 cup firmly packed brown sugar
1/2 cup granulated sugar
2 eggs
1 teaspoon pure vanilla extract
1 1/2 cups all purpose flour (or 1 cup all purpose and 1/2 cup whole wheat flour)
1 teaspoon baking soda
1 teaspoon ground cinnamon
3 cups oatmeal, uncooked
1 cup raisins (optional)
1/2 cup dandelion petals

1. Preheat the oven to 350 degrees F. If using the raisins, pour into a bowl and cover with water; set aside.

2. In a mixing bowl, cream together the butter and sugars. Stir in the eggs and vanilla. Stir in the flour. Stir in the baking soda and cinnamon. Stir in the oats.

3. If using the raisins, drain them and fold into the batter.

4. Fold in the dandelion petals a tablespoon at a time until well mixed.

5. Drop the dough by rounded tablespoonfuls onto a baking sheet and bake 8 to 10 minutes, or until the edges are golden. Remove from the oven and cool on the sheet for 1 minute. Transfer to a wire rack and cool completely.

Makes about 4 dozen cookies.

Dandelion Flower Fizzy Drink

Here's a fun and unique beverage for parties. It is mildly alcoholic.

4 cups dandelion flower heads (green parts still attached)
10 ½ cups water
5 cups granulated sugar
Juice and rind (white pith removed) from 2 lemons

1. Pour the water into a pot and bring to a boil.

2. Pour the flower heads into a large bowl, then pour the hot water over them. Cover and refrigerate overnight.

3. Line a sieve with a double layer of cheesecloth or some coffee filters and strain the flower and water mixture.

4. To the resulting liquid, add the sugar, juice, and rinds.

5. Pour the mixture into a pot and place over medium heat. Stir until the sugar dissolves.

6. Strain and pour into pitchers or bottles. Store, unrefrigerated, for 4 weeks before drinking.

Adapted from a recipe at NibblingOnNature.blogspot.com.

Lacto-Fermented Dandelion Soda

Lacto-fermented foods have many health benefits, including increased nutrition and pro-biotics.

Starter:
1 inch + of fresh ginger, with skin, grated
1 tablespoon + sugar
2 cups unchlorinated water
1 tablespoon blackstrap molasses

For the Soda:
About 5 cups dandelion flower heads (if desired, you may use just the petals)
1/3 cup granulated sugar

1. Place the ginger and sugar into a glass quart jar. Add the water and stir. Add the molasses and stir.

2. Secure a piece of cloth over the jar with a rubber band or string. Set in a warm location. Stir twice a day; add a teaspoon of sugar and a little grated ginger once a day. By day 2 or 3, the mixture should be bubbling before you stir it.

3. Once the starter is bubbling, gather the dandelion flowers.

4. Fill a pot with water and bring to a boil.

5. Warm a 1 quart jar by running hot tap water over it. Place the flowers or petals in the jar. Pour the hot water into the jar, filling it nearly to the top. Secure the jar's lid. Let sit for 24 hours.

6. Strain through a fine sieve lined with coffee filters, pressing down on the flowers. Pour the resulting liquid into a saucepan.

7. Place the saucepan over medium high heat and add the sugar. Stir until the sugar completely dissolves. Remove from the stove and allow to come to room temperature.

8. Add ¼ cup of the starter for every quart of dandelion flower liquid. Cover with a cloth and let sit for 3 days. Every 12 hours, stir the mixture. Every day, taste the mixture. If it seems bitter, add a little sugar. By day 3, the drink should be bubbly.

9. Bottle the soda and seal jars. Store 24 hours before drinking. If you store longer than 24 hours, move to the refrigerator or the jars may burst.

Adapted from a recipe at ALifeUnprocessed.blogspot.com.

Simple Dandelion Flower Fritters

When I first served these to my family, they were very skeptical. In fact, I had a hard time getting them to taste even one. But once they did, they were hooked! Flower fritters are a really delicious – and addictive - way to eat dandelion flowers.

Olive oil
A couple of handfuls of dandelion flower heads
1 egg
1 cup milk
1 cup all purpose flour

1. Place a skillet over medium high heat and add enough oil to come up the sides of the pan just a little.

2. In a bowl, whisk the egg. Add the milk and flour, stirring until well blended.

3. Dip a flower in the batter, coating completely, and place it flower side down in the hot oil in the skillet. Repeat until the skillet is full of dipped flower heads. Cook until the batter is crispy, then turn the flowers over with tongs (or forks) and cook the opposite side. It's important to fully cook the batter on the flowers so it's crispy, not mushy.*

5. As each flower finishes cooking, transfer it to paper towels to drain.

* If desired, add an inch of oil to the skillet, so the flowers are immersed in the oil when cooking. If this method is used, you won't need to turn over the flowers.

Spicy Dandelion Flower Fritters

2 – 3 handfuls of dandelion flower heads
Olive oil
1 ¼ cups all purpose flour
Salt
Pepper
2 teaspoons ground cumin
2 teaspoons ground coriander
1 turmeric
1/3 cayenne
1 teaspoon baking powder
Water

1. Place a skillet over medium high heat and add enough oil that it comes barely up the sides of the pan.

2. In a bowl, whisk together the flour, a little salt and pepper, cumin, coriander, turmeric, cayenne, and baking powder. Add a little water, stirring to combine, until the mixture is the consistency of pancake batter.

3. Dip a flower in the batter, coating completely, and place it flower side down in the hot oil in the skillet. Repeat until the skillet is full of dipped flower heads. Cook until the batter is crispy, then turn the flowers over with tongs (or forks) and cook the opposite side. It's important to fully cook the batter on the flowers so it's crispy, not mushy.*

5. As each flower finishes cooking, transfer it to paper towels to drain.

* If desired, add an inch of oil to the skillet, so the flowers are immersed in the oil when cooking. If this method is used, you won't need to turn over the flowers.

Cornmeal Dandelion Flower Fritters

Olive oil
2 or 3 cups of dandelion flower heads
1 egg
1 cup milk
1/4 cup all purpose flour
1 cup cornmeal
Salt
Pepper

1. Place a skillet over medium high heat and add the oil.

2. In a bowl, whisk the egg. Add the milk, flour, and cornmeal, stirring to combine. Season with salt and pepper.

3. Dip a flower in the batter, coating completely, and place it flower side down in the hot oil in the skillet. Repeat until the skillet is full of dipped flower heads. Cook until the batter is crispy, then turn the flowers over with tongs (or forks) and cook the opposite side. It's important to fully cook the batter on the flowers so it's crispy, not mushy.*

5. As each flower finishes cooking, transfer it to paper towels to drain.

* If desired, add an inch of oil to the skillet, so the flowers are immersed in the oil when cooking. If this method is used, you won't need to turn over the flowers.

Beer Battered Dandelion Flower Fritters

1 cup all purpose flour
1/2 tablespoon baking powder
Salt
1/2 bottle of beer
About 2 cups dandelion flower heads
Olive oil

1. Place a skillet over medium high heat and add the oil.

2. In a bowl, stir together the flour, baking powder, and a pinch or two of salt. Stir in the beer until well blended.

3. Dip a flower in the batter, coating completely, and place it flower side down in the hot oil in the skillet. Repeat until the skillet is full of dipped flower heads. Cook until the batter is crispy, then turn the flowers over with tongs (or forks) and cook the opposite side. It's important to fully cook the batter on the flowers so it's crispy, not mushy.*

5. As each flower finishes cooking, transfer it to paper towels to drain.

* If desired, add an inch of oil to the skillet, so the flowers are immersed in the oil when cooking. If this method is used, you won't need to turn over the flowers.

Dandelion "Mushroom" Fritters
Many people feel these fritters taste like mushrooms.

½ cup coconut oil
1/4 cup all purpose flour
¼ cup cornmeal
Salt

Garlic powder
Onion powder
Pepper
Dried Parmesan cheese
Cayenne pepper
Olive oil

1. Combine the flour, cornmeal, a pinch of salt, a pinch of garlic powder, a pinch of onion powder, a little pepper, a pinch of dried Parmesan, and a pinch of cayenne pepper in a bowl. Set aside.

2. Place about an inch of oil into a skillet.

3. Rinse the flowers in a strainer.

4. Once the oil is hot, shake off a flower and dip it into the flour mixture, covering it completely. Place the dipped flower in the hot oil and brown on all sides. Repeat with the remaining flowers

5. Drain on paper towels.

Dandelion Petal Pancakes

Kids will love this recipe because it takes a familiar food and adds some fun to it by adding dandelion petals.

3/4 cup all purpose flour (or half whole wheat flour and half all purpose flour)

1/4 cup cornmeal
1/2 cup + milk
1 egg
Petals from 30 dandelion flower heads
Salt
Olive oil spray

1. In a small mixing bowl, combine the flour and cornmeal. Stir in the milk and egg. Fold in the flower heads and season with a little salt. If the batter seems too thick, add a bit more milk.

2. Spray a skillet with olive oil and place over medium high heat. Once hot, add a couple of spoonfuls of the batter. Cook until golden, then flip and cook the opposite side.

Cheesy Dandelion Petals

Oil
1 egg
1 cup all purpose flour
3/4 cup milk
1/2 teaspoon white vinegar
1 teaspoon granulated sugar
Salt
1/2 teaspoon baking soda
1 teaspoon baking powder
Salt
2 cups dandelion petals
1 cup grated Cheddar cheese
1 cup cooked fresh or frozen corn
1/4 chopped fresh chives

1. Place a skillet over medium high heat and cover the bottom with oil.

2. Whisk an egg in a mixing bowl. Stir in the flour, milk, vinegar, sugar, baking soda, and baking powder. Add a pinch or two of salt.

3. Fold in the dandelion petals, breaking up any clumps. Fold in the cheese, corn, and chives.

4. Drop the mixture by tablespoonfuls into the hot oil in the skillet. When one side is golden, turn and cover another side. Transfer to paper towels to drain.

Serves 2.

Dandelion Drop Biscuits

2 cups all purpose flour
2 + ½ teaspoon baking powder
½ teaspoon salt
1 teaspoon finely diced dried chives
5 tablespoons cold butter, cut into small pieces
1 cup milk
½ cup dandelion petals

1. Preheat the oven to 450 degrees F.

2. Stir together the flour, baking powder, salt, and chives. Add the butter, working it into the mixture with your hands until it resembles coarse crumbs.

3. Stir in the milk. Fold in the petals. The batter should be sticky.

4. Scoop out ¼ cup of batter and drop it onto a baking sheet. Repeat with the remaining batter, putting biscuits about 2 inches apart.

5. Bake until the edges start to brown, about 12 minutes.

Makes about a dozen.

Candied Dandelion Flowers

Eat candied flowers alone as a sweet treat, or use them to decorate cakes, cupcakes, and cookies.

Dandelion flower heads
Powdered (confectioner's) sugar

1. Preheat the oven to 350 degrees F.

2. Pour some powdered sugar into a bowl. Dredge the flowers in the sugar so they are completely covered. Shake off any excess.

3. Place the flowers on a baking sheet and bake in the preheated oven for 5 minutes. Remove from the oven and allow to cool a bit. Dust with more sugar.

Coconut Dandelion Blossom Muffins

2 cups all purpose flour
2 teaspoons baking powder
1/2 teaspoon salt
1 cup loosely packed dandelion petals
1/4 cup coconut oil (or olive oil)
1/4 cup pure honey
1 egg, beaten
1 1/2 cups milk
1 tablespoon cocoa powder
1 teaspoon cinnamon
1 teaspoon pure vanilla extract
1/3 cup coconut flakes

1. Preheat the oven to 400 degrees F. Line a muffin tin with paper cups, or grease each cup. Set aside.

2. In a large mixing bowl, stir together the flour, baking powder, and salt. Fold in the petals, breaking up any clumps.

3. In another bowl, stir together the milk, honey, oil, and egg.

4. Form a well in the center of the flour mixture and pour the milk mixture into it. Stir until just combined. The batter will be lumpy.

5. Pour the batter into the prepared muffin tin and bake until a toothpick inserted into the center of a muffin comes out clean, about 20 – 25 minutes. Remove from the stove and allow to cool for 5 minutes in the pan. Transfer muffins to a wire rack to cool completely.

Makes about 14 muffins.

Variation: Pour batter into a greased loaf pan and bake for 25 - 30 minutes, or until a toothpick inserted into the center comes out clean.

Adapted from a recipe at NaturesNurtureBlog.com.

More Muffin Ideas

Dandelion petals can be added to almost any muffin recipe.

Dandelion Flower Syrup

Use this syrup just like any other sweet syrup – on pancakes and waffles.

Petals from about 250 dandelion flower heads
Juice from 1 lemon
8 cups water
5 cups granulated sugar

1. In a large pot placed over medium high heat, add the petals, juice, and water. Bring to a boil. Reduce the heat to medium low. Cover and simmer for 60 minutes.

2. Remove the pot from the stove. Cover and let stand overnight.

3. Line a sieve with cheesecloth or coffee filters and strain the mixture, discarding the flowers.

4. Clean the pot and pour the liquid back in it. Place over medium high heat and add the sugar, stirring constantly until dissolved. Bring to a boil.

5. Reduce the heat and simmer for another 60 minutes, or until the mixture is as thick as maple syrup.

6. Warm a glass jar (ideally a canning jar) by running hot tap water over. Pour out any water and pour the syrup into the jar. Cap.

Dandelion Petal "Veggie" Burgers

1 cup packed dandelion petals
1/2 cup all purpose flour
1/2 cup quick cooking oats
2 tablespoons bread crumbs
2 tablespoons freshly grated Parmesan cheese
1/2 cup finely chopped onions
1/2 teaspoon garlic powder
1/4 teaspoon basil
1/4 teaspoon oregano
1/2 teaspoon cumin
Salt
Pepper
Cayenne pepper flakes
1 egg, beaten

1/4 cup milk
Olive oil

1. In a large mixing bowl, combine the dandelion petals, flour, oatmeal, bread crumbs, parmesan, onion, garlic powder, basil, oregano, cumin. Stir in salt, pepper, and Cayenne pepper flakes to taste.

2. Stir in the egg and milk. The batter should be sticky. Shape the batter into 4 or 5 patties.

3. Place a tablespoon oil in a skillet and warm it over medium high heat. Add a patty and cook it until crisp and golden on one side. Flip and cook the opposite side.

4. Serve as is, or use in place of a beef hamburger patty.

Serves 4 – 5.

Adapted from a recipe at NaturesNurtureBlog.com.

Dandelion Hearts

Dandelion hearts are my name for the center of the dandelion plant before it sends up stems and flowers. The flowers are stored in the heart of the dandelion, waiting for weather warm enough to shoot up and bloom. Once cooked, the heart is similar in flavor to artichokes.

1 dandelion plant, dug up from the soil*

Dab of butter

Salt

Pepper

1. Remove the dandelion leaves and store for future use.

2. If desired, carefully peel or cut away the dark green outer part of the heart of the plant, revealing the mass of yellow at the center.

3. To a pot with a steamer insert, add water. Place over medium high heat.

4. Once the water comes to a boil, add the dandelion heart, cover, and steam until tender.

5. Season with a dab of butter, salt, and pepper.

* NOTE: Some people prefer to use a serrated grapefruit spoon or pocketknife to cut the heart right out of the plant without digging it up.

Dandelion Petal Sorbet

Here's a fantastic way to try dandelions for the first time. Many people have a hard time believing dandelions make good desserts, but this recipe proves them, wrong, wrong, wrong!

3 cups water
1/2 cup granulated sugar
1/2 cup pure honey
4 cups dandelion petals
3 tablespoons freshly squeezed lemon juice

1. Pour the water, sugar, and honey into a saucepan. Place over medium heat. As soon as it comes to a boil, remove from the stove and stir in the petals. Cover and allow to sit for 60 minutes.

2. Line a sieve with a double layer of cheesecloth or some coffee filters and strain the mixture.

3. Stir in the lemon juice. Refrigerate until completely chilled.

4. Pour into an ice cream maker and follow the manufacturer's directions for sorbet. Freeze for at least 3 days before eating.

Adapted from a recipe at Food.com.

Dandelion Flower Bread

Dandelion petals are very mild-tasting, so you probably won't notice them in this bread - unless you look hard. But the flower petals in the recipe add great nutrition!

2 cups unbleached flour
2 teaspoons baking powder
1/2 teaspoon salt
2 cups dandelion petals
1/4 cup olive oil
4 tablespoons pure honey
1 egg
scant 1 1/2 cups milk

1. Preheat the oven to 400 degrees F. Grease a loaf pan; set aside.

2. In a large mixing bowl, stir together the flour, baking powder, and salt. Fold in the petals, breaking up any clumps.

3. In a separate bowl, combine the oil, honey, egg, and milk.

4. Make a well in the center of the flour mixture and pour in the oil mixture. Stir until just combined. The batter will be lumpy. Pour into the prepared loaf pan.

5. Bake for 25 minutes, then check for doneness by inserting a toothpick in the center of the loaf to see if it comes out clean. If it doesn't, keep baking for up to 40 minutes, checking for doneness periodically.

Makes 1 loaf.
Adapted from a recipe at ImperfectlyDelicious.blogspot.com

Simple Dandelion Wine

Recipes for dandelion wine go back centuries. There are literally thousands of variations, but this cookbook includes some of the easiest. The finished drink is a sweet dessert wine.

8 cups dandelion flowers
9 cups granulated sugar
Freshly squeezed juice from 4 oranges
Freshly squeezed juice from 3 lemons
1 packet champagne or wine yeast (or dry active yeast)

1. Pour 1 gallon of water into a pot and place over high heat. Bring to a boil.

2. Pour the dandelion flowers into another large pot. Pour the hot water over them. Cover and allow to sit for 3 days.

3. Strain the mixture in a colander lined with cheesecloth.

4. Pour the liquid into a clean pot and add the sugar. Stir until completely dissolved. Stir in the orange and lemon juice.

5. Pour ½ cup of lukewarm water into a small bowl. Add the yeast; stir. Allow to sit until foamy, about 5 to 10 minutes.

6. Add the yeast mixture to the dandelion liquid. Stir.

7. Pour the mixture into large jars. Place the open end of a balloon over the opening in the jars. As the wine ferments, the balloons will fill with air. Twice a day, check on the wine, releasing air from the balloons as needed. Allow to ferment for 6 weeks, or until the balloons no longer fill with air.

8. Strain the wine through a double layer of cheesecloth. If you prefer clear wine, without sediment, strain as much as needed. Bottle.

Makes about 4 quarts.

Spiced Dandelion Wine

2 1/2 teaspoons yeast
1/4 cup warm water
8 cups dandelion petals
16 cups water
1 cup freshly squeezed orange juice
3 tablespoons freshly squeezed lemon juice
3 tablespoons freshly squeezed lime juice
8 whole cloves
1/2 teaspoon ground ginger
3 tablespoons chopped orange peel
1 tablespoon chopped lemon peel
6 cups granulated sugar

1. Pour the yeast and ¼ cup of lukewarm water into a bowl. Set aside.

2. Pour the water into a large pot. Add the petals, orange, lemon, and lime juice. Stir in the cloves, ginger, peels, and sugar. Place the pot over medium high heat and stir until the sugar dissolves.

3. Bring to a boil and allow to boil gently for 60 minutes.

4. Line a sieve with cheesecloth and strain, throwing away the solids. Allow the liquid to cool.

5. When the liquid is no longer hot, but is still warm, stir in the now foamy yeast mixture. Allow the mixture to stand overnight.

6. Pour the mixture into bottles, left uncorked. Place the open end of a balloon over the opening in the jars. As the wine ferments, the balloons will fill with air. Twice a day, check on the wine, releasing air from the balloons as needed. Allow to ferment for 3 weeks, or until the balloons no longer fill with air. Cork and store bottles in a cool location.

Makes about 4 quarts.

Pink Dandelion Wine

8 cups dandelion petals
8 cups boiling water
Juice from 3 lemons
3 1/2 cups granulated sugar
10 oz. frozen, sweetened raspberries
1 yeast cake

1. Warm a gallon jar by running hot tap water over it. Pour out any water and place the petals in it. Pour boiling water over them and allow to stand overnight.

2. Line a sieve with cheesecloth and strain.

3. Pour the liquid into a pot and add the juice. Add the raspberries and sugar. Bring to a boil over medium high heat, then simmer for 20 minutes.

4. Pour the mixture into the now-clean, pre-warmed jar, allowing it to cool until it's lukewarm. Add the yeast, stirring until dissolved. Cover and place in an out of the way location for 10 days, or until the hissing ceases.

5. Line a sieve with two layers of cheesecloth and strain the liquid into the cleaned-again jar. Allow to stand for 3 days.

6. Line the sieve with fresh cheesecloth and strain again. Pour the liquid into bottles, left uncorked. Cap the bottles the following day. Allow to age for several months before consuming.

Makes 4 - 5 bottles.

Dandelion Mead

Mead is an ancient alcoholic beverage. Because it's made with honey, dandelion flowers – with their mild, honey-like flavor – are a natural addition.

12 cups dandelion petals
4 lbs. pure honey
22 cups water
3 tablespoons freshly squeezed lemon juice
1 cup freshly made, strong black tea
6 whole cloves
1 cinnamon stick, crushed
2 tablespoons dry yeast

1. Pour the petals into a crock or food grade bucket.

2. In a large pot, pour the honey and 8 cups water. Bring to a boil over medium high heat and boil for 3 minutes. Pour the mixture over the petals.

3. Stir in the juice, tea, cloves, and cinnamon.

4. Pour the remaining water into the pot and bring to a boil over medium high heat. Pour into the crock. Allow to cool enough to become lukewarm.

5. Add the yeast. Cover with plastic wrap and allow to stand for 7 days.

5. Line a colander with two layers of cheesecloth and strain the mixture, discarding the solids. Pour the liquid back into the crock

and cover with tightly. Let stand for at least 2 months. Bottle, covering the openings with fabric held in place with string or rubber bands, and let stand for 3 days before corking. Allow to age for at least 2 months before consuming.

Dandy Cordial

A cordial is a sweet, alcoholic drink, traditionally consumed after dinner.

1 1/2 cups water
3 cups dandelion petals
1 cup granulated sugar
Peel from 1 lemon, sliced into thin strips
3 cups vodka

1. Pour the water and the petals into a saucepan placed over medium high heat. Bring to a boil, then reduce the heat to medium and simmer for 3 minutes.

2. Remove the pan from the stove, cover, and let stand for 10 minutes.

3. Line a sieve with two layers of cheese cloth or some coffee filters and strain.

4. Add the sugar, place the pan over low heat, and stir until the sugar is completely dissolved.

5. Remove from the stove and add the lemon peel and vodka.

6. Warm a glass jar (ideally a canning jar) by running hot tap water over it. Pour out any water. Pour the vodka mixture into the jar and seal tightly. Refrigerate for up to 2 weeks, shaking every few days. Serve cold, shaking well just before pouring.

Makes about 7 - 8 pints.

Dandelion Buds:
Tasty Morsels

The young, unopened flowers of the dandelion – the buds – are just as edible as every other part of this amazing plant. For best results, catch the buds while they are tightly closed.

Flavor

Some people compare the flavor of dandelion buds to mushrooms. Others say they taste like honey. Others find them bitter. The latter are eating the green parts surrounding the bud (the sepals), which are, indeed bitter. As for the other varying ideas on the taste of the bud – well, much depends on how they are prepared.

When to Harvest Dandelion Buds

Pick buds while they are still tightly closed and rounded – not oval-shaped and beginning to open. Remove the bitter sepals (the crown of green "leaves" on the stem-end of the bud) before using.

Preserving Dandelion Buds

Dandelion buds may be preserved through freezing or, short term, through pickling. (Please see the pickled dandelion recipes in this section.)

Freezing: Place buds in a single layer on a rimmed baking sheet. Put the baking sheet in the freezer. Once the buds are hard and frozen, transfer them to a freezer bag. Use within 6 months for recipes calling for cooked buds.

Asian-Style Pickled Dandelion Buds

Pickled dandelion buds have an almost cult-like following. Here I provide several recipes to choose from.

1 cup dandelion buds
1/2 cup purple onion, minced
3 tablespoons minced fresh ginger
5 garlic cloves
apple cider vinegar
soy sauce or tamari

1. In a pint jar with a plastic lid, pour the buds, onion, ginger, and garlic cloves.

2. Fill the jar halfway with vinegar. Fill to just below the rim with soy sauce. Cover with the plastic lid* and refrigerate for 3 weeks before eating.

* Metal lids react negatively with vinegar and therefore should not be used.

Adapted from a recipe from MethowValleyHerbs.com.

Old Fashioned Pickled Dandelion Buds

Dandelion buds
Dandelion vinegar (or apple cider vinegar)

1. Place the dandelion buds in a glass jar and cover with the dandelion vinegar. Cover with a plastic lid* and refrigerate for 2 weeks before eating.

* Metal lids react negatively with vinegar and therefore should not be used.

Simple Pickled Dandelion Buds

1 cup dandelion buds
½ teaspoon sea salt
½ teaspoon granulated sugar
White wine vinegar

1. Place the buds in a glass bowl; toss with the salt and sugar until well coated.

2. Pour the buds into a glass jar with a plastic lid.* Pour the vinegar over the buds. Secure the lid. Refrigerate for 2 weeks before eating.

* Metal lids react negatively with vinegar and therefore should not be used.

Italian-Style Dandelion Buds

2 tablespoon sea salt
1/2 cup dandelion buds
White wine vinegar
2 teaspoons granulated sugar
2 bay leaves
3 sprigs fresh thyme

1. Pour 1 cup of water into a small saucepan. Add the salt and bring to a boil over medium high heat.

2. Place the buds in a non-reactive bowl and pour the salt water over them. Cover and allow to sit at room temperature for 3 days.

3. Drain. Pour the buds into a glass jar (ideally a canning jar) with a plastic lid.*

4. Place a non-reactive saucepan over medium heat and add the vinegar, sugar, bay leaf, and thyme. Bring to a boil. Run hot tap water over the outsides of the jar, then pour the vinegar mixture over the buds. Allow the jar to cool naturally to room temperature.

5. Secure the jar's lid and refrigerate for 2 weeks before eating.

* Metal lids react negatively with vinegar and therefore should not be used.

Pickled Dandelion Buds and Juniper Berries

2 teaspoons sea salt
1 cup dandelion buds
5 juniper berries
5 whole allspice
5 black peppercorns
1 clove garlic
1 cup dandelion vinegar, white wine vinegar, or apple cider vinegar

1. Pour 1 cup of water into a saucepan. Add the salt and bring to a boil over medium high heat.

2. Run hot tape water over a glass jar (ideally, a canning jar); remove any water. Place the buds into the jar and pour the salt water over them. Allow to cool to room temperature. Cover and refrigerate for 3 days.

3. Strain. In a clean jar, pour the buds, juniper berries, allspice, peppercorns, and garlic.

4. Pour the vinegar in a clean saucepan and bring to a boil over medium high heat. Run hot tap water on the outside of the jar, then pour the vinegar over the dandelion bud mixture, covering completely.

5. Let the jar cool completely, then secure a plastic lid* on the jar and refrigerate for 2 weeks before eating.

* Metal lids react negatively with vinegar and therefore should not be used.

Dill Pickled Dandelion Buds

4 cups dandelion buds
1 teaspoon sea salt
1 garlic clove, crushed
1 cup white vinegar
¼ cup packed brown sugar
1 cup water
2 tablespoons dill seed
4 whole cloves

1. Pour the buds in a saucepan and cover with water. Place over medium heat and bring to a boil. Boil for 5 minutes. Drain. Pour the buds into a sterile glass jar (ideally, a canning jar).

2. In a non-reactive saucepan, pour the vinegar, sugar, water, salt, doll, garlic, and cloves. Bring to a boil over medium high heat and boil for 10 minutes. Run hot tap water over the outsides of the jar, then pour the vinegar mixture over the dandelion buds. Allow to come to room temperature.

3. Place a plastic cap on the jar* and refrigerate for at least 2 weeks before eating.

* Metal lids react negatively with vinegar and therefore should not be used.

Boiled Dandelion Buds

Dandelion buds
Salt
Pepper
Garlic powder
Onion powder
Freshly grated Parmesan cheese

1. Pour the buds into a saucepan and cover with water. Place over medium heat and bring to a boil. Gently boil until tender, about 20 minutes. Drain.

2. Season with salt, pepper, garlic powder, and onion powder. Top with freshly grated Parmesan cheese, if desired.

Variation: Boil the buds, drain, then drizzle with olive oil and a little vinegar.

Adapted from a recipe from CloverleafFarmBlog.com.

Beer Battered Dandelion Buds ("Dandelion Popcorn")

When I first encountered this recipe, it seemed really bizarre. But then I remembered how wonderful battered and fried dandelion flower fritters are. Dandelion buds are, after all, just unopened flowers. Some people call these battered and fried buds "popcorn" because they are an addictive, crunchy, salty snack.

Tightly closed dandelion buds, stems removed
1 egg

1 cup milk
1 cup all purpose flour
Coconut oil
Salt

1. Fill a bowl with cold water. Add the buds and soak for 30 minutes. Drain and pat dry.

2. In a mixing bowl, whisk the egg. Whisk in the milk. Stir in the flour and mix well.

4. Melt some coconut oil in a skillet placed over medium high heat. You'll need enough oil that it comes up an inch along the sides of the skillet. Bring the oil to 375 degrees F.

5. Dip a handful of buds into the batter, coating completely. Place in the hot oil. Shake the skillet and cook until golden.

6. Remove the buds with a slotted spoon and drain on paper towels. Repeat step 5 until all the buds are fried.

7. If desired, salt the finished buds.

Dandelion Bud Omelet

1 ½ tablespoons butter
1 cup dandelion buds
¼ cup minced onion
4 eggs
3 tablespoons milk
1 tablespoon chopped fresh parsley
Salt
Pepper

1. In a skillet placed over medium heat, melt the butter. Add the dandelion buds and sauté for 3 minutes. Transfer to a bowl using a slotted spoon.

2. In a large bowl, whisk the eggs and milk together. Stir in the parsley. Season with salt and pepper.

3. Pour the mixture into the skillet. Add the prepared buds, sprinkling on top of the egg mixture. Cook until eggs are done, about 3 or 4 minutes.

4. Fold the omelet in half and serve.

Serves 1.

Dandelion Bud and Chicken Stir Fry

5 ½ tablespoons butter
1 cup dandelion buds
2 boneless, skinless chicken breast, sliced into thin strips
1 garlic clove, minced
4 green onions (scallions), sliced thin
1 bell pepper, diced
½ a head of bok choy, sliced into thin strips
Low sodium soy sauce
Olive oil

1. Place a skillet or wok over medium heat. Add the butter; when it's fully melted, add the buds. Sauté until tender, about 8 minutes. With a slotted spoon, transfer to a bowl.

2. If needed, add a little olive oil to the skillet. When very hot, add the chicken; sauté until cooked through.

3. Add the green onions, bell pepper, and bok choy; sauté until tender. Return the buds to the skillet.

4. Sprinkle some soy sauce onto the mixture. Taste; if needed, add more. When the meat is cooked through and the vegetables are tender, serve as is, or over rice.

Serves 2.

Split Pea and Dandelion Bud Soup

1 cup split peas, cooked in water or stock, according to package
directions (do not drain)
1 teaspoon salt
6 cups water
2 tablespoons butter
½ cup onions, minced
4 garlic cloves, minced
½ cup thinly sliced celery
2 cups dandelion buds
½ teaspoon dried basil
½ teaspoon dried sage
1 cup milk

1. In a skillet placed over medium high heat, melt the butter. Add the
onions, garlic, celery, buds, basil, and sage. Sauté until the
vegetables are tender and the onion translucent.

2. Stir the bud mixture into the split pea mixture. Bring to a simmer
over medium heat and simmer for 30 minutes.

3. Stir in the milk and cook until warmed through.

Serves 2 – 4.

Dandelion Stems: Nature's Noodles

Stems are probably the least eaten part of the dandelion plant. Most frequently, they are found as a garnish in green salads, but there are other ways to eat them, too – including as a replacement for flour noodles.

Flavor

Dandelion stems are bitter, but less so when cooked.

When to Harvest Dandelion Stems

Cut the stems (rather than pulling them) at the base of the plant. Look for the lightest green stems you can find. Snip off the buds.

Preserving Dandelion Stems

Dandelion stems may be preserved by freezing.

Freezing: First cut the stems to the desired length. Lay in a single layer on a rimmed baking sheet and place in the freezer. When the stems feel hard and frozen, transfer to a freezer bag. Use within 6 months, in recipes calling for cooked stems.

Dandelion Stem Noodles

Here's a dish your guests will never be able to identify! Remember that dandelion stems are quite bitter and that you should taste them in between boilings until you are satisfied their bitterness is sufficiently reduced.

Young dandelion stems
Salt
Pepper
Freshly grated or powdered Parmesan cheese

1. Fill a pot with water and a couple of pinches of salt and place over medium high heat. Bring to a boil and add the dandelion stems. Cook until tender, but not mushy, about 10 minutes. Stems should be bright green. Drain.

2. Taste the stems. If they seem too bitter to you, fill the pot with fresh salted water, bring to a boil, and add the stems again. Boil for another minute or two, then drain.

3. Pour the stems into a serving bowl. Season with salt and pepper. Sprinkle with Parmesan cheese. Toss to combine.

Dandelion Stem Spaghetti

Spaghetti sauce
Browned ground beef (optional)
Salt
Young dandelion stems

1. In a large saucepan, pour the spaghetti sauce and browned beef, if using. Place over medium low heat and gently warm. Do not allow to bubble.

2. Fill a pot with salted water and place over medium high heat. Bring to a boil and add the dandelion stems. Boil until stems are tender, but not mushy. Drain.

3. Pour the stems into the spaghetti sauce, stir well, and serve.

Variation: Cook traditional spaghetti noodles and drain. When stirring the spaghetti into the sauce, also stir in cooked dandelion stems.

Dandelion Roots:
Great Nutrition, Great Flavor

The roots of dandelions are a great source of vitamins C, A, D, B complex, and beta-carotene. They are also high in iron, potassium, zinc, biotin, phosphorus, and magnesium and are a good antioxidant.

Traditionally, dandelion roots were used as medicine – for cleansing the liver and gallbladder, and a tonic against PMS and general malaise. Today, many people still drink dandelion root tea for these reasons. In cooking, the plant's roots are most commonly treated like parsnips.

Flavor
Young spring roots, especially when cooked, taste similar to salsify or artichoke hearts. Older, larger roots are more bitter, but boiling or roasting reduces or removes their bitterness. When dandelion roots are roasted, they taste very much like coffee.

When to Harvest Dandelion Roots
Fall is considered the best time to gather dandelion roots; at that time of year, the roots have had all spring and summer to store nutrients that will feed the plant through the winter – and these nutrients will feed you, too. But you may collect roots any time of year. When the roots will be lightly cooked, most people prefer less bitter, spring roots.

Buying Dandelion Roots

Some health food stores sell dehydrated dandelion roots, primarily for making tea or as a coffee substitute.

Preserving Dandelion Roots

Dandelion roots may be preserved through freezing, dehydrating, or dry roasting. (See the dry roasting recipe in this chapter.)

Freezing: Scrub the roots well with a vegetable brush. Fill a clean sink or bowl with ice water and bring a pot of water to a boil. Add the roots and boil for 1 minute. (For roots that are quite large, chop first.) Immediately drain and dump into the ice water. Once completely cool, drain well. Pat dry and place in freezer bags. Use within 6 months or so.

Dehydrating: Scrub the roots well with a brush, then chop. Dehydrated dandelion roots are very hard, and since they are mostly used for making tea (and therefore must be ground before using), it's important to chop them into small pieces of about the same size. Fat roots should be halved or quartered. Place on the tray of a dehydrator set at 135 degrees F. Dehydrate until there is no trace of moisture or softness in the roots. Alternatively, place on a wire cooling rack set on top of a rimmed baking sheet; place in the oven, set at its lowest temperature, until thoroughly dry. Allow to completely cool, then place in an air tight container in a cool, dry, dark location.

How to Dig Up Dandelion Roots

Wait until the soil is moist – after a good rain is best. (If no rain is in the forecast, use a sprinkler to moisten the soil before digging.) Using a long screwdriver or a dandelion puller, insert the tool in the soil, near the base of the plant. Pull toward you. Repeat a few more times until you can pull up the entire plant. It will be difficult to get the entire root out of the soil - but that's fine. It will ensure a new crop next year.

Dry-Roasted Dandelion Root

Use this recipe to remove the bitterness of older dandelion roots, and for recipes calling for roasted roots.

Fresh dandelion roots

1. Preheat the oven to 250 degrees F.

2. Place the roots in a single layer on a rimmed baking sheet. Place in the preheated oven with the door left ajar. Stir every 15 minutes until roots are shrunk, crunchy, and golden, about 2 – 3 hours.

3. To store, allow the roots to completely cool. Place in an air tight container in a cool, dry, dark location.

Dandelion Root Cake

When roasted, dandelion roots loose their bitterness and take on a coffee-like flavor. That is their contribution to this cake: Coffee flavor, minus the caffeine, and plus lots of nutrients.

1 cup quick-cooking tapioca
1 cup hazelnuts, roasted and ground in a food processor or coffee grinder
1 cup almond meal*

1 1/2 teaspoon baking powder
1/2 teaspoon baking soda
1/2 teaspoon salt
1 teaspoon cream of tartar
1 cup milk
3 tablespoons chopped, roasted dandelion roots
2 eggs
1 cup pure maple syrup
1/2 cup coconut or olive oil
2 teaspoons pure vanilla

1. Preheat the oven to 350 degrees F. Grease a 9 inch cake pan; set aside.

2. In a mixing bowl, stir together the tapioca, hazelnuts, almond meal, baking powder, baking soda, salt, and cream of tartar.

3. In a small saucepan placed over medium high heat, pour the milk and the dandelion roots. Bring to a boil. Turn off the heat and allow the mixture to sit for 10 minutes. Strain.

4. Beat the eggs in another mixing bowl. Add the milk, syrup, oil, and vanilla and mix well. The batter will be thinner than the average cake batter.

5. Bake in the preheated oven until a knife inserted in the center comes out clean, about 40 minutes.

* You can make this yourself by grinding almonds in a coffee grinder or food processor until a flour forms.

Makes one 9 inch cake.

Adapted from a recipe at dyhanaverse.blogspot.com.

Sautéed Dandelion Roots

1 tablespoon olive oil or bacon drippings
Fresh spring dandelion roots, sliced
1 onion, diced
2 garlic cloves, minced

1. Pour the oil in a skillet placed over medium high heat. Once warm, add the root, onion, and cloves. Sauté until the roots are tender and the onions translucent.

Serves 1 – 2.

Dandelion Root Meat Rub

2 tablespoons dehydrated dandelion root
2 teaspoons onion powder
2 teaspoons garlic powder
1 tablespoon cumin
Salt
Pepper

1. In a coffee grinder, grind the dandelion roots into a fine powder.

2. Pour the powder into a bowl and stir in the onion powder, garlic powder, and cumin. Add a little salt and pepper. Mix well.

3. Rub into beef or wild game and allow to stand for half an hour before cooking.

Adapted from a recipe at HungerAndThirstForLife.blogspot.com.

Toasted Dandelion Root Marinade

8 tablespoons fresh spring dandelion root, chopped
1 teaspoon juniper berries
1 teaspoon ground coriander
1 teaspoon ground cinnamon
1 whole clove
1 cup packed brown sugar
1 cup kosher salt
4 cups whole milk

1. Place a skillet over medium heat. Add the dandelion root and toast, stirring frequently to prevent burning.

2. Just before the roots are done, add the berries, coriander, cinnamon, and clove. Stir until dark brown.

3. Add the sugar, kosher salt, and whole milk. Remove from the stove.

4. Use the mixture as a marinade for beef or wild game.

Dandelion Roots in Tomato Sauce

To visualize this recipe, imagine eating parsnips with tomatoes. Then pick the youngest dandelion roots you can find.

Fresh spring dandelion roots, cut into 1 inch long pieces
Salt
1 onion, diced
1 tablespoon olive oil
Small can tomato sauce
Pepper
Oregano

1. Fill a saucepan with water and place over medium high heat. Add a pinch or two of salt. Bring to a boil. Add the dandelion roots and cook for 15 minutes. Drain.

2. Place a skillet over medium high heat. Add the oil. Once warmed, add the onion and sauté until translucent.

3. Add the roots and sauté until tender and golden, about 10 minutes.

4. Add the tomato sauce, stirring to mix well. Season with salt, pepper, and a pinch or two of oregano.

Serves 2.

Pickled Dandelion Root

A big handful of fresh spring dandelion roots, chopped
3 garlic cloves
2 teaspoons ground ginger
¼ cup tamari
About 3 ½ cups apple cider vinegar

1. In a glass quart-sized jar, pour the roots, garlic, ginger, and tamari.

2. Pour vinegar over the mixture, until it comes within ¼ inch of the top of the jar.

3. Secure a plastic lid* on the jar and refrigerate for 3 weeks before eating. Eat alone, or add to salads or soups

* Metal reacts negatively with vinegar, so be sure to use a plastic lid.

Roasted Dandelion Root & Other Root Vegetables

Fresh spring dandelion roots, chopped into pieces of about the same size
Other root vegetables (such as parsnips, carrots, and potatoes), cut into approximately the same size
Olive oil
Salt
Pepper
1 garlic clove, minced (optional)
2 sprigs of fresh rosemary or thyme (optional)

1. Preheat the oven to 450 degrees F.

2. Place the roots and vegetables in a bowl and toss with olive oil until they are well coated. Season with salt and pepper. Add the minced garlic and rosemary or thyme, if using.

3. Place the roots and vegetables in a single layer on a rimmed baking sheet. Roast, stirring once in a while, until the vegetables and root are golden and tender, about 45 minutes.

Boiled Dandelion Roots

Fresh dandelion roots, chopped into 1 inch pieces
Butter
Salt
Pepper

1. Fill a saucepan with salted water. Place over medium high heat and bring to a boil.

2. Add the roots and boil until they can easily be pierced with a fork.

3. Season with a dab of butter and a little salt and pepper.

Dandelion Root "Coffee"

This drink tastes just like instant coffee – but it has much more nutrition and no caffeine.

Dry roasted dandelion roots
Water

1. Fill a small saucepan with water and place over medium high heat. Bring to a boil.

2. In the meantime, grind the roots in a coffee grinder until they form a power. Add the powder to the boiling water, reduce the heat and simmer for 10 – 15 minutes. Strain.

Dandelion Root Chai Tea

1 tablespoon dry roasted dandelion root
2 cinnamon sticks, broken into pieces
5 cardamom pods, crushed
1 teaspoon whole cloves
1 teaspoon whole black peppercorns
1 inch piece of fresh ginger, sliced thin
4 cups water
Milk
Pure honey (optional)

1. Place a 2 quart saucepan on the stove. Add the roots, cinnamon, cardamom, cloves, peppercorn, and ginger. Cover with water and turn the heat to medium high. Bring to a boil. Reduce heat and simmer for 15 minutes. Strain through a fine sieve.

2. Fill about 3/4 a cup with the mixture, then pour in milk. Sweeten with honey, if desired. Store remaining chai liquid in the refrigerator for up to 2 weeks.

Roasted Dandelion Root Ice Cream

For years, I avoided dandelion root ice cream recipes because I just couldn't imagine they would taste good. Finally, when I got up the nerve to try some, I realized how wrong I was! This ice cream has hints of coffee and yes, even peanut butter, in it.

2 1/2 cups heavy cream
1 1/2 cups half and half
1 1/4 cups granulated sugar
1/2 cup finely ground, dry roasted dandelion roots
5 egg yolks

1. In a double boiler, pour the cream, half and half, and sugar. Turn the heat to medium and stir until the sugar dissolves. Bring to a very gentle simmer.

2. Add the dandelion root powder. Simmer gently for 45 minutes. Strain.

3. In a pot, whisk the eggs. Turn the heat to medium. A little at a time, add the cream mixture. Stirring once in a while, cook gently until thickened enough that it coats the back of a spoon. Strain. Chill.

4. Pour into an ice cream maker and follow the manufacturer's directions.

Hint: If you have a favorite coffee ice cream recipe, substitute ground, dry roasted dandelion roots for coffee granules, or "dandelion coffee" for brewed coffee.

Dandelion Root Tea

There is no doubt dandelion root tea is bitter. I began drinking it as a remedy for PMS. (Some drink it as a diuretic, or digestion improver, or liver and gallbladder cleanser. Some people also feel it improves blood sugar levels.) Over time, I grew to crave the flavor, but you can make the tea less bitter by filling half the tea ball with dandelion roots and the other half with a sweeter herb, like red raspberry leaf.

Dehydrated dandelion roots
Water

1. Fill a small saucepan with water. Bring to a boil over high heat.

2. In the meantime, use a coffee grinder to finely chop the dehydrated dandelion roots. (Try not to let the roots get powdery. If they do, cut a double piece of cheesecloth into a square and place the powder in the center; pull up the edges of the square and tie them with kitchen string. Place inside a cup.) Fill a tea ball with the chopped roots and place the tea ball in a cup.

3. Once the water boils, pour it over the tea ball. Steep 10 minutes. Over-stepping will result in a very bitter tea.

Dandelion Root Beer

Believe it or not, dandelion roots have long been used to make root beer. This recipe nods back to this old fashioned, non-alcoholic drink.

For the starter:
1 teaspoon diced fresh dandelion roots
2 teaspoons granulated sugar (or real honey or pure maple syrup)

For the root beer:
10 medium sized fresh dandelion roots
1 cup pure maple syrup
1 cup real honey
¼ cup freshly squeezed lemon juice

1. In a pint jar, pour the 1 teaspoon diced roots and 1 teaspoon sugar. Pour 1 cup of water over them. Put a paper towel over the top of the jar (securing with a rubber band or a piece of string) and set aside for 2 days.

2. Add another teaspoon of sugar and re-cover. By day 3, the starter should be bubbly.

3. Place the 10 roots in a pot and cover with water. Bring to a boil over medium heat and gently boil for 1 hour. Remove from the stove and allow to sit overnight. Strain.

4. Pour 1 cup maple syrup and 1 cup honey into a one gallon jar. Add the dandelion root liquid, the starter, and the lemon juice. Stir well. Cover and allow to sit for 24 hours before drinking.

Dandelion Beer

This alcoholic drink is similar to those found in 19th century cookbooks.

½ lb. young dandelion roots
1 gallon water
1 lemon, peel removed and the pith (white part) cut away
½ fresh ginger root, peeled and crushed
1 lb. light brown sugar
1 oz. cream of tartar
1 tablespoon yeast
4 teaspoons light brown sugar

1. Pour the 1 lb. of sugar and the cream of tartar into a food grade bucket. Set aside.

2. In a large pot placed over medium heat, place the roots, ginger, and water. Add the lemon rind and bring to a boil. Boil for 10 minutes. Remove from the stove and allow to cool slightly.

3. Strain the root mixture into the bucket, stirring until the sugar completely dissolves. Allow to cool to room temperature.

4. Add the juice from the lemon; stir. Sprinkle in the yeast. Cover and allow to rest in a warm location for 3 days or until it completely stops bubbling and fermenting.

5. Strain. Bottle, adding ½ teaspoon brown sugar to each pint. Set aside until the beer clears (about 7 days).

About the Author

Kristina Seleshanko is a cook, gardener, writer, mom, and wife. One of her favorite jobs was working as a research librarian for *Gourmet* magazine. But she'd rather freelance at home – for publications such as *Woman's Day* and *Backwoods Home* - and tend to her garden and her family. Kristina is the author of 18 books, plus many ebooks. She blogs about cooking, gardening, God, and more at **ProverbsThirtyOneWoman.blogspot.com**.

Other Books by the Author

A Vegetable for Every Season Cookbook: We all know we should eat more vegetables. But how can we cook all those vegetables in the most delicious way possible? *A Vegetable for Every Season Cookbook: Making Veggies Easy & Delicious* is the answer. Whether you get your vegetables garden fresh, from the farmer's market, or from the grocery store, this cookbook will guide you to over 155 delicious recipes you can make with them, from mashed cauliflower and grilled eggplant to crispy stir fried green beans and stuffed pumpkin to zucchini tots and carrot oatmeal cookies. PLUS you'll get tips for growing vegetables yourself, clues about what each vegetable tastes like, and a wide variety of health, cooking, and gardening ideas to inspire you to healthier eating and living.

Starting Seeds: This step by step guide offers everything you need to know to start vegetables, herbs, and other edibles from seed. Includes complete information on:

* How to choose a seed starting method
* How to winter sow
* How to indoor sow
* How to direct sow
* How to transplant seedlings
* How to save seeds for years
* How to make your own seed starting pots from recycled materials
* How to make your own durable plant markers from recycled materials

and more.

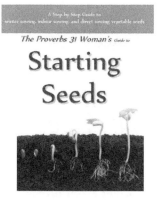

Find more books by Kristina at

www.ProverbsThirtyOneWoman.blogspot.com

Printed in France by Amazon
Brétigny-sur-Orge, FR

14187015R00090